CRIMINOLOGY AND CRIME PREVENTION

ACKNOWLEDGEMENTS

I want to thank everyone who made this book possible: first of all, my partner, and Plod (my tortoise) who have put up with endless conversations about deadlines, content and pretty much anything to do with this book including the occasions when I have locked myself upstairs to get it done.

Secondly, this book would not have been possible without the support received from Critical Publishing. Lily and Julia combined have dragged me through the process of writing my first book, with their words of wisdom, advice and explaining how everything works. Without them I would still be clueless and thinking 'how hard can it be?'

Thanks to Tony Blockley for editing this book and providing me with his suggestions throughout. His LinkedIn post is the sole reason for how this came about and I have really enjoyed this experience – even with its challenges.

Finally, I want to say thanks to those in policing who have helped me throughout my career to date. There have been so many people who have moulded me to who I am today, got me through the difficult points and have been an extended family to me. Their insight and guidance will stick with me throughout my life.

James Dickety, 2023

To order our books please go to our website www.criticalpublishing.com or contact our distributor Ingram Publisher Services, telephone 01752 202301 or email IPSUK.orders@ingramcontent.com. Details of bulk order discounts can be found at www.criticalpublishing.com/delivery-information.

Our titles are also available in electronic format: for individual use via our website and for libraries and other institutions from all the major ebook platforms.

CRIMINOLOGY AND CRIME PREVENTION

THE PROFESSIONAL POLICING CURRICULUM IN PRACTICE

JAMES DICKETY

SERIES EDITOR: TONY BLOCKLEY

CRITICAL PUBLISHING

First published in 2023 by Critical Publishing Ltd

All rights reserved. No part of this publication may be reproduced, stored in a retrieval system, or transmitted in any form or by any means, electronic, mechanical, photocopying, recording or otherwise, without prior permission in writing from the publisher.

The author has made every effort to ensure the accuracy of information contained in this publication, but assumes no responsibility for any errors, inaccuracies, inconsistencies and omissions. Likewise, every effort has been made to contact copyright holders. If any copyright material has been reproduced unwittingly and without permission the Publisher will gladly receive information enabling them to rectify any error or omission in subsequent editions.

Copyright © 2023 James Dickety

British Library Cataloguing in Publication Data
A CIP record for this book is available from the British Library

ISBN: 978-1-915080-74-5

This book is also available in the following e-book formats:
EPUB ISBN: 978-1-915080-75-2
Adobe e-book ISBN: 978-1-915080-76-9

The right of James Dickety to be identified as the Author of this work has been asserted by him in accordance with the Copyright, Design and Patents Act 1988.

Text design by Greensplash
Cover design by Out of House Limited
Project management by Newgen Publishing UK

Critical Publishing
3 Connaught Road
St Albans
AL3 5RX

www.criticalpublishing.com

Printed on FSC accredited paper

CONTENTS

About the series editor and author — vi

Foreword by the series editor — vii

Introduction: every contact leaves a trace — 1

Chapter 1: Crime, victimisation and harm — 5

Chapter 2: Offenders and the causes of offending — 23

Chapter 3: Procedural justice — 47

Chapter 4: Policing, social control and the role of other agencies — 59

Chapter 5: Policing and politics: accountability, police powers and their regulation — 75

Chapter 6: Principles of crime prevention — 93

Chapter 7: Policing approaches — 111

Sample answers — 135

References — 142

Index — 158

ABOUT THE SERIES EDITOR

TONY BLOCKLEY

Tony Blockley is the lead for policing at Leeds Trinity University, responsible for co-ordinating policing higher education, including developing programmes and enhancing the current provision in line with the Police Education Qualification Framework (PEQF) and supporting the College of Policing. He served within policing for over 30 years, including a role as Chief Superintendent and Head of Crime.

ABOUT THE AUTHOR

JAMES DICKETY

James Dickety has worked in policing for over 10 years as a special constable, police constable and now as a detective within CID. He has been involved in neighbourhood policing teams, response teams and operations and within investigations. His key interest is developing knowledge within the service and bridging the gap between academia and policing. James has a degree in criminology and criminal justice from the University of Portsmouth and has studied at both undergraduate and Master's level in policing policy and leadership.

FOREWORD

Police professionalism has seen significant developments over recent years, including the implementation of the Vision 2025 and the establishment of the Police Education Qualification Framework (PEQF). There is no doubt that policing has become complex, and that complexity and associated challenges increase day by day with greater scrutiny, expectation and accountability. The educational component of police training and development therefore allows officers to gain a greater understanding and appreciation of the theories and activities associated with high-quality policing provision.

The scholastic element of the Vision 2025 provides an opportunity to engage in meaningful insight and debate around some of the most sensitive areas of policing while also taking the lessons of the past and utilising them to develop the service for the future. While there are many books and articles on numerous subjects associated with policing, this new series – The Professional Policing Curriculum in Practice – provides an insightful opportunity to start that journey. It distils the key concepts and topics within policing into an accessible format, combining theory and practice to provide you with a secure basis of knowledge and understanding.

Policing is now a degree-level entry profession, which has provided a unique opportunity to develop fully up-to-date books for student and trainee police officers that focus on the content of the PEQF curriculum, are tailored specifically to the new pre-join routes and reflect the diversity and complexity of twenty-first-century society. Each book is stand-alone, but they also work together to layer information as you progress through your programme. The pedagogical features of the books have been carefully designed to improve your understanding and critical thinking skills within the context of policing. They include learning objectives, case studies, evidence-based practice examples, critical thinking and reflective activities, and summaries of key concepts. Each chapter also includes a guide to further reading, meaning you do not have to spend hours researching to find that piece of information you are looking for.

This book explores some of the basic principles associated with policing and provides underpinning knowledge for police officers undertaking their duties. The introduction of some criminological theories provides a better understanding of why people offend, thereby putting you in the shoes of the offender; after all, crime and criminality are not always straightforward. Examining the criminal justice system (CJS) and procedural justice allows you to consider the role of policing and the ethical considerations you will undoubtedly have to make. This of course links into the everyday challenges of police accountability and how this expectation manifests itself within your practice. The final chapter considers the principles of crime prevention and provides some crucial thoughts combining prevention and criminological theory, appreciating the principal role of policing is the prevention and detection of crime. Within the book there are many helpful topics and opportunities to create greater in-depth understanding, allowing for widening knowledge and education.

Having been involved in policing for over 40 years, the benefits of these books are obvious to me: I see them becoming the go-to guides for the PEQF curriculum across all the various programmes associated with the framework, while also having relevance for more experienced officers.

Professor Tony Blockley
Discipline Head: Policing
Leeds Trinity University

INTRODUCTION: EVERY CONTACT LEAVES A TRACE

For a book about criminology and crime prevention you may wonder why it starts with a phrase instantly associated with forensic science. The notion of 'every contact leaves a trace' is, however, about more than just forensics; although its origin cannot be disputed, the phrase can be relevant to any point in your policing career and is potentially one of the best pieces of advice I ever received.

Before talking about the contents of this book it is worth discussing the realities of policing. Throughout your career you are likely to come across some traumatic incidents, some angry people, problems that are seemingly unsolvable and inevitably you will interact with those who are potentially at their lowest point in life. While this introduction examines how you can impact on others, remember that every one of these contacts you have will leave a trace on you and at times you may need support. This is not because you are weak but because you are human; everyone needs support from time to time. You will find a couple of helpful resources listed at the end of this introduction should you ever need them.

Most sections of the public rarely meet the police, but when they do that contact is of vital importance. Some people use that single interaction as the basis for their ideas and opinions of the police service. This perception can dictate whether they will call the police in the future or encourage their friends/family to do so, or even whether they will interact with you in any capacity. The police service cannot function without public information and interaction, and therefore you must remember the importance of caring for the public. You may not realise it at the time, but your singular contact can have an impact on a future officer's interaction with the member of the public and they could be dealing with a murder investigation or high-risk missing person where often time is in short supply. Your earlier contact will leave a trace on that person so make sure where possible it is a positive one.

Knowing about criminology and crime prevention will not instantly make you a 'super-cop' and turn these interactions around. But when applied correctly it might make your contact with the public less of a trace event and more impactful – which at a time when the service is stretched can have untold benefits.

The contents of this book will also not stop crime from happening at all; you will see in the first two chapters that crime can take place for a myriad of reasons and not every intervention can tackle every single reason. But by knowing what works and where, you can take an informed approach to what you might want to do based on the knowledge you already have.

To help build this bank of information, I have briefly explained the contents of each chapter and how it might impact upon your work.

Chapter 1 discusses crime, victimisation and harm, which includes how crime is recorded in England and Wales, explores why people are potentially victimised and introduces you to victimology. One benefit to your practice could be being able to identify common issues early on in your interaction with someone and therefore referring them to the support they need and more importantly preventing them from becoming a victim again. You might wonder why crime recording is important, but with data comes analysis, and if you are able to record data accurately and know the differences between the two methods of recording crime you can use and understand them in your practice. These topics are also often subject to discussion in the media, and you can therefore be better placed to dispute often misleading or partially informed headlines.

Chapter 2 examines offenders and introduces you to a range of criminological theories that attempt to explain why people offend. Being able to apply these models of offending and understanding that no one model is perfect might mean you are able to put in place innovative bail conditions or map offending patterns in a different light, making interventions and investigations more effective.

Chapter 3 discusses procedural justice, which is a topic everyone in policing should understand. While there are well-established expectations that you will act ethically, procedural justice goes beyond that and explains how you should display your decision making to those you serve to ensure they remain on side and do not feel aggrieved by the process. This will help with support you receive from the public and hopefully minimise the resistance you receive to any decisions you make.

Chapter 4 moves to a slightly broader look at your policing practice and focuses on social control and how policing fits into this within the CJS. It is important to understand the roles of other agencies within policing and the CJS as there are times where you will need to work alongside others, and you can minimise effort and maximise results by correctly utilising each organisation.

Chapter 5 discusses police accountability, powers and their regulation. Policing rightly has to police by consent. This means we must be accountable to the public and this is done through several different means. This chapter explains those mechanisms and explores how they fit into your practice. Sometimes criticism from the public can be frustrating for those in policing, but it can also be of benefit to the service and this chapter explains how that is the case.

The penultimate chapter, Chapter 6, discusses principles of crime prevention. It helps you understand the step between criminological theory and your practice and how the two intertwine.

The final chapter builds on the principles of crime prevention and discusses policing approaches such as hot spot policing and problem-oriented policing. You will see throughout your practice that various approaches to policing come in and out of favour. While they all have both benefits and pitfalls, this chapter analyses these approaches and their application so you can use them within your practice.

By the end of this book, you will understand the value of knowing about criminology and crime prevention in your practice. You do not need to be an expert, but hopefully you will finish with sufficient grounding to positively affect your work and maximise your impact on the public.

FURTHER READING

www.policecare.org.uk/
Police Care UK. This charity supports former and current police officers through psychological and physical harm, which they may have experienced while policing. Their support is extensive and personalised to the individual so if you need support all you have to do is reach out. They are also a charity so if you are looking for a good cause to support, they are a great policing option.

www.oscarkilo.org.uk/
Oscar Kilo – The National Police Wellbeing Service is the national body of police wellbeing, providing a lot of strategic products for those on the front line as well as wellness checks, mindfulness apps and information sessions on sleep to name a few. They will not provide direct help to individuals, but their services help signpost people and aim to limit people from getting so horrendously sick that they cannot continue in their service.

CHAPTER 1
CRIME, VICTIMISATION AND HARM

LEARNING OBJECTIVES

AFTER READING THIS CHAPTER YOU WILL BE ABLE TO:

- explain what crime is;

- know how crime is measured in England and Wales;

- understand victim risks and vulnerability;

- know why some experience repeat victimisation;

- explore the relationship between victims and offenders and how restorative justice can help long term.

INTRODUCTION

This chapter looks at a wide range of areas studied in the initial stages of a criminal justice degree and topics you should be aware of when you start policing. Victims and witnesses should always be at the centre of your practice; you will require their involvement throughout any criminal trial and often success depends upon them. As such, it is vital you are able to understand them and any vulnerabilities they have. By knowing and understanding some of the reasons people become repeat victims you maximise your chances of providing a suitable intervention and in the long term hopefully cutting crime. Finally, this chapter looks at restorative practice. This can be seen dismissively by those in service; however, when you read about the potential impacts it has on crime you will see how it can be beneficial for policing.

WHAT IS CRIME?

The question 'what is crime?' sounds straightforward but the more you investigate the question the complexity really starts to show. The online Cambridge dictionary, for example, has three different definitions: the first being '*illegal activities*' (Cambridge University Press, nd). As we examine each definition, they are all problematic to some extent. If you have ever studied law, you will be aware of the range of things that are prohibited by law and are therefore illegal, but would you expect a police officer to deal with all of them as a crime?

Victim Support, a charity that supports those affected by crime, suggests that crime is a '*deliberate act that causes physical or psychological harm, damage to or loss of property, and is against the law*' (Victim Support, nd). Using this definition is also, however, problematic as it suggests that some harm has to be caused. An example where this could be an issue is a car without the correct depth on the tyres which does not constitute a crime under the above definition, but yet is an offence dealt with by policing.

Becker (1963), a sociologist who examined deviance, argues that crime or deviances are created by social groups who make the rules and when these are broken, a crime occurs. In essence, crime takes place when it is seen by society to have taken place. However, this is also problematic as it has been previously stated that a law needs to be broken. There are many things that cause public offence and outrage, yet despite that much of it is not a crime.

Utilising a hybrid of definitions to describe crime might be beneficial. You could describe crime as a deliberate act or omission prohibited by law, which could or will cause harm, whether physical or psychological, or an act that has been proven to potentially cause harm if not addressed. This definition addresses several issues. Firstly, some definitions fail to mention that a law needs to be broken to constitute a crime. Secondly, the latter part addresses the offences that may not have directly caused harm. An example is a drunk driver who managed to get home without incident, but there is an evidence base to show why that behaviour should be against the law.

REFLECTIVE PRACTICE 1.1

LEVEL 5

Having read the above, answer the following.

- What is your definition of crime?

- How can the inclusion of an indication of harm become problematic?

- Consider both graffiti and the works of famous artists such as Banksy; both are classified as criminal offences but yet one is seen as valuable. How much do you think social construct contributes towards what is and is not seen as a crime?

Definitions by their very nature can be troublesome as there is always some sort of outlier or exception to the rule. In policing, definitions are important to know and understand so you are able to go about your duty and facilitate the correct support for victims of crime. 'What is crime?' is often a good initial essay title when you start studying so knowing and understanding what it is will be helpful. If you are new to criminological study, it is also a good area to begin researching as you will begin to explore the complexity of this social science.

CRITICAL THINKING ACTIVITY 1.1

LEVEL 4

Another area with various definitions is domestic abuse. Research a number of different agencies (police, Crown Prosecution Service (CPS) or support services as examples) in relation to this.

- How does each agency define domestic abuse?

- Does each definition mean certain behaviours are included or excluded?

- How do these definitions compare with the cross-government definition?

- What problems does this cause?

- When working jointly, do differing definitions cause other problems?

- If so, what can be done to counter this and allow effective partnership working?

HOW DO WE MEASURE CRIME?

Crime in England and Wales is measured in two distinct ways: police recorded crime and the Crime Survey for England and Wales (CSEW).

Police recorded crime is exactly that – on attendance or on report of an incident, the police log what crimes have taken place and do so according to the Home Office Counting Rules (HOCR). The HOCR include lists of definitions for each offence and different categories, which does not always mean recorded crime matches legal definitions. For example, at the time of writing (January 2023), burglary is separated into dwelling and non-dwelling as well as distraction breaks; the latter are burglaries that take place while the home owner is distracted usually by an accomplice pretending to do door-to-door sales or asking for a glass of water (Home Office, 2022). This separation is often used when the Home Office want to know how prevalent certain crime styles or modus operandi (MO) are or monitor performance in certain crime types. Equally these rules can be used for political gain; the rules are updated every year and as such it could be argued that definitions are altered to help show a drop in crime or a rise depending on the need at the time.

In addition, not all offences that are reported get recorded. This is because for each report one principal offence generally gets recorded and is done so according to the HOCR. Generally, violent crimes get recorded above acquisitive crimes. In some cases, crimes such as stalking also get an additional crime recorded regardless of what offences it is combined with. This means that the police recorded crime picture can be incomplete, and the rules could be manipulated to highlight issues or show improvements in areas if there was a desire to do so. There are, however, safeguards in place to prevent forces from manipulating this for their gain as this is often subject to review by the HMICFRS (His Majesty's Inspectorate for Constabularies and Fire and Rescue Services).

As well as the discussed issues with the HOCR, there is also the key issue that some people decide not to report matters to police. This could be for several reasons and you will come across people who fear the police, historically have had issues or do not trust them. People may also have personal pressures preventing them from reporting, meaning that none of these offences while clearly still happening will never reach the police recorded statistics. This unrecorded number is referred to as the dark figure of crime.

REFLECTIVE PRACTICE 1.2
LEVEL 4

Imagine a time when you have spoken to someone and despite them wanting to tell you something there were clearly barriers in the way of them doing so.

- What tactics did you use to encourage that engagement?

- Did you try and connect with them on an emotional level and if so, how? If not, how would you?

- Imagine you now had this engagement as an officer, would your role or uniform add another barrier? Explain your answer.

- How would you counter that?

The CSEW was created to help counter the issue of the dark figure of crime. This survey is completely independent from the police and administrated by a government department. It has most recently been conducted on the phone due to Covid-19. Historically, however, it was conducted in person with its most recent typical sample size of around 3000 houses a month. This survey is seen as a more reliable way of measuring crime given its broad data set and can be used to map out trends more effectively.

CRITICAL THINKING ACTIVITY 1.2

LEVEL 5

Consider the sample size for the CSEW. Do you think that is enough to represent the entire population of England and Wales?

What criteria would you want to be included to ensure as representative a sample as possible?

Sample answers are provided at the end of this book.

Figure 1.1 compares the two data sets on a relatively common crime, bicycle theft, between 1981 and 2017. You can see that police recorded crime, the bars at the bottom, does not cover the same volume of offences the CSEW captures.

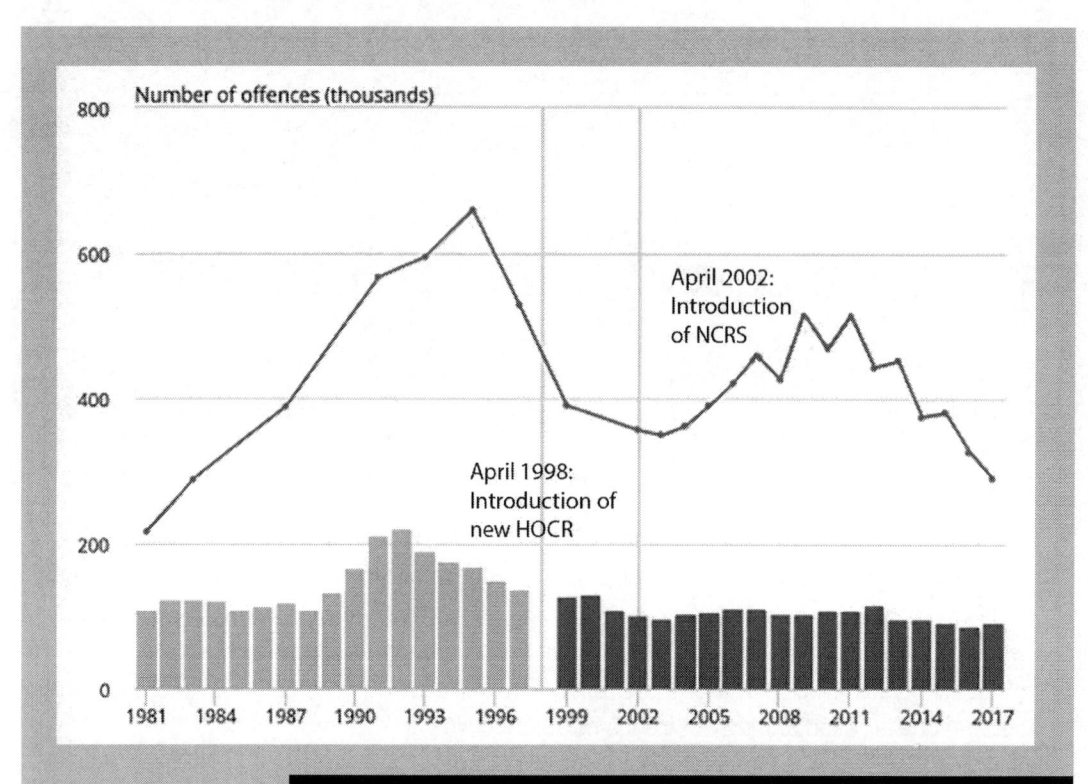

Figure 1.1 Graph comparing the CSEW and police recorded crime (Office for National Statistics, 2017)

The CSEW does have limitations, for example it does not survey businesses and as such shoplifting is completely ignored and it cannot effectively map issues such as possession of drugs, which typically have no victim and as such would not be mentioned by the sample (Office for National Statistics, 2022). As a result, the only real data set for these offences is the police recorded crime figure.

CRITICAL THINKING ACTIVITY 1.3

LEVEL 6

Consider the two types of government measurement of crime.

- What do you think are the benefits of each type?

- How should the police use each data set?

- Should the police handle each data set differently? If so, how and why?

ARE THERE ANY OTHER WAYS TO MEASURE CRIME?

Measuring crime in the volume of incidents, however, does not give a full picture. Crime as you hopefully know by now affects victims in so many different ways and while each crime might be referred to as a singular incident depending on the crime type, the impact to individuals could be vast. A simple example could be comparing two thefts – the impact of a theft of a parsnip from a corner shop, while still a crime, does not compare with a theft of a priceless piece of art from a museum. Despite that, however, they both still only equate to one incident each.

The British Transport Police (BTP) have a unique position in British policing. While crime still takes place on the railway, would a better measure of crime in their jurisdiction be the impact it has on those that pay for its services and the rail operators? As an example, as a result of police-related activity on the railway in the reporting year 2019–20, the railway was delayed approximately 2,174,591 minutes. While this can be argued as overly simplistic and the BTP's role in policing is more than that, could it be seen as a valid measure of crime for them as a force?

In relation to County Lines, the rail network is vital in moving operators around, and while the crimes may not have taken place in their area, the BTP County Lines Task Force has arrested over 926 people (British Transport Police, 2021). While this does not claim to be a measure of crime itself, for organised criminality especially where identifiable victims are difficult to locate, arrests or other measures of police activity such as disruptions may be a good measure to see its prevalence. This is problematic as it relies on the police, for example, to attribute the incident to the specific MO or even identify that the disruption is linked to something bigger, but it could be a start especially as this crime type is unlikely to feature on other measurements of crime.

In the same way as measuring crime on the railway by the minutes of disruption caused, a similar suggestion could be made for fraud. This crime type is one of the biggest recorded offences in England and Wales, but that fact alone does not provide us with an illustration of its impact, especially when it so rarely hits the news. It is estimated that fraud costs the UK economy £137 billion each year (Gee and Button, 2021) and, to use another example, one fraud MO alone with data recorded over just five months cost users of WhatsApp a total of £1.5 million (Action Fraud, 2022). These numbers quantify the impact on the economy more than the measure of X offences per 1000 in the population and is more relevant to the crime type.

As you can see, measuring crime can be more complex than simply counting the number of police reports. When it comes to your practice or any future research it is important that you utilise a broad data set in order to fully understand the impact of your chosen crime type.

VICTIM RISKS, VULNERABILITIES AND REPEAT VICTIMISATION

When it comes to repeat victimisation, victim risks and vulnerabilities, this is an area likely to cause you frustration within your service. When it comes to policing, you will often deal with people who you feel will not take basic steps to keep themselves safe. However, after reading this section you will appreciate why this may be the case and may then be able to encourage interventions, which will lessen demand on policing longer term.

DOMESTIC ABUSE

A common example where you will see repeat victimisation is in the area of domestic abuse and due to its very nature, this has large numbers of repeat victimisation. Farrell et al

(1995) argue that the reason for this is that this offence type requires little effort on behalf of the offender. They argue that this is due to there being a lack of other capable guardian(s) at the victim's home and a lack of restrictions of access to the address and, conversely, there are few other options for the victim to escape, hence why there is an emergence of refuges. They also argue that, as the nature of offending continues, the victim realises that they are physically overpowered and as such there is little merit in continuing to resist. When attending a domestic situation in the future, consider these factors when talking to the victim even when a criminal justice outcome may not be forthcoming.

This is, however, just a singular theory of why domestic abuse experiences repeat victimisation. There is a plethora of research and reading material available including trauma informed theories, which might provide a different perspective on domestic repeat victimisation. As domestic abuse constitutes a large proportion of police calls and while this book may not have the space to explore the subject fully, it is strongly recommended that policing has a sound knowledge and understanding of the issue.

COMMON VULNERABILITIES WITH REPEAT VICTIMS

One psychological explanation for repeat victimisation could be being due to a trauma response. Following a violent event, it is possible that individuals experience a response that could result in avoidance behaviours, intrusions (such as flash backs), negative moves or states or thinking and hyperarousal such as over thinking. As a result of this trauma-based response, victims' behaviours may mean that they become more likely to expose themselves to risky situations, which in turn means they are likely to become victimised again (Graham-Kevan et al, 2015).

Another theory argues that self-control is a contributory factor. Gottfredson and Hirschi's (1990) theory argued that those who lack self-control tend to dislike settings that require discipline. As a consequence, they engage in behaviours consistently and disregard what consequences they bring (Turanovic and Pratt, 2014) and as such by associating in these undisciplined settings they naturally expose themselves to victimisation. Equally this self-control argument also applies to offenders as it does victims, in that they are attracted to places of little discipline and as such they can succumb to their urges to offend. In Gottfredson and Hirschi's original paper, a lot of weight was put onto the parental upbringing being the reason why these individuals lack self-control and even in later books following scrutiny on the theory, where others had raised cultural differences, the authors still referred to how different cultures raise their children (Buker, 2011).

Shorrock et al (2020) in their study reviewed repeat victims, which were reported to the multi-agency safeguarding hub (MASH) in an English policing area. They discovered that in

75 per cent of the cases they reviewed, mental health was associated and in 40 per cent drugs, alcohol or a combination of the two were present. This highlights how external factors can impact on victimisation and as such while some matters may not be seen as policing issues, early referral or highlighting to other agencies could save a person from being victimised in the future.

POLICING SPOTLIGHT

A classic example of where a victim's vulnerabilities have led to their repeated victimisation is the case of Fiona Pilkington, which happened in 2009. She killed herself and her daughter in a lay-by of the A47 by setting their car on fire. Fiona's daughter was disabled and had the mental age of a four-year-old and their death was as a direct result of repeated incidents and a failed police response (BBC News, 2011).

Her family reported 33 times to police regarding harassment including stones and eggs being thrown at Fiona's house and on one occasion her daughter was told to lift her night-dress while her brother was locked in a shed at knife point.

Despite the range of reports police only attended on eight occasions and the police's failure to identify Fiona and her family as vulnerable was a core reason that led to their death, according to a review conducted (Independent Police Complaints Commission, 2009).

Another factor that impacts on victimisation according to a range of studies is the demographics of the victim themselves. Tseloni and Pease's (2003) study found that the risk of victimisation increased 40 per cent when you are a man compared with a woman. Single, divorced and widowed people faced 39, 132 and 38 per cent more personal crimes than those who were married, and lone parents experienced 77 per cent more crimes than other people. They also found similar impacts depending on income, urbanisation of the area residing in and number of cars.

The same study also found that certain behaviours impacted on whether someone becomes a victim. As an example, if you shopped daily rather than never you were 73 per cent more likely to experience crime and if you were out every evening compared with just one evening it increased 33 per cent. Those who use public transport saw increases of up to 56 per cent if they used it more than once a week. Routine activity theory is discussed in the next chapter, and it might be worth considering these risk factors when it is discussed to see how that theory interacts.

Another concept is that of 'event dependency'. In a study focusing on burglary, it was explained that the victim is more likely to be selected if they have recently been a victim of the same crime. In the eyes of the offender, it is argued that if there were three addresses, one known as unsuitable to burgle, one possibly suitable and one known to be suitable it makes sense for the offender to offend at the address they know is the least risk (Johnson, 2008). Another paper utilised crime data and found that if a household was subject to a burglary incident in the previous four years, their odds of being burgled were 68 per cent higher than others. Also, if the victim was previously assaulted, the chances of their household being subjected to property crime increased by 70 per cent (Ellingworth et al, 1997).

THE LINK BETWEEN VICTIMS AND OFFENDERS

While criminological theories have provided some explanation as to repeat victimisation another aims to place the blame of becoming a victim with the victim. In Wolfgang's (1958) study, he reviewed homicide cases and discovered that in 26 per cent of cases the victim had a role in the instigation of violence. Controversially, Amir (1971) in his study of rape linked victim participation to 19 per cent of cases he reviewed and while this area of work has been largely discredited, we can still see it as mitigation in court today (Goodey, 2005; Gray and Horvath, 2018).

EVIDENCE-BASED POLICING

Despite the criminological theory being discredited it is important to understand and recognise that these thoughts still exist as they can be seen in policing practice today. Sleath and Bull (2017) conducted a study on policing attitudes about rape and the impacts this has upon cases, utilising studies into rape from around the world including America, England and Wales and Norway.

They found that on the occasions where the victim was intoxicated due to alcohol, more blame was attributed to the victim than the offender. Additionally, in cases of acquaintance rape, the victims were more likely to be blamed than in a stranger rape.

When it came to officer impact, the studies found that male officers were significantly more likely to blame the victim than female officers although if they were specially trained this did not impact on their levels of victim blaming.

These attitudes are still reported in policing practice today; for example, in a recent HMICFRS report, a victim of rape was quoted as saying:

The police [officer] was quite rude to me. That wasn't very nice. She was implying that I was making it up. It was just her whole attitude to things

(HMICFRS, 2021b)

Despite victim blaming theories being discredited, it is evident it still appears in policing practice today, which justifies the emergence of projects such as Operation Bluestone to improve police responses to rape. As this project is ongoing, not all documents are available to the public; however, an overview is available at: www.college.police.uk/research/projects/operation-soteria-bluestone.

REFLECTIVE PRACTICE 1.3

LEVEL 5

Think about a recently talked about rape case in the media or if you cannot think of one research a case where the defendants were found not guilty.

- Reflect on the comments made in public forums about the case or between your friends/family – how many of them were victim blaming?

- Given that often the full details are not reported, how can this discourse be challenged?

- What impact do you think the discourse about the case has on the victim and their future likelihood to report cases to the police?

The offender/victim overlap should not, however, be excluded due to a victim blaming theorist. A more recent study discovered that adverse childhood experiences (ACEs), which are discussed in Chapter 2, were commonly found in both victims and offenders. It also found that victimisation and offending both peak in adolescence.

A study based in America reviewed the relationship between victim and offenders in murder cases over four years. It found that in 46 per cent of cases both parties were acquaintances, 12 per cent of these were friends, 12 per cent romantic links and 18 per cent were strangers. Acquaintances were people that they had short interactions with, not enough to define them as friends; for example, they may be in a criminal enterprise together or neighbours. The paper argues that these people know each other enough to have disputes but not enough to become friends, which is why they typically had a high proportion of murders (Decker, 1993).

Murder is not the only crime that has shown a link between victim and offenders. A study into modern day slavery showed that many victims are first enticed through pursuing a romantic interest. Many suspects show affection towards the victims as well as organising places for them to live, bringing them food or providing transportation. Most of the suspects started living with the victims and at this point they were encouraged to enter prostitution and then give the suspect the money so they could assist with 'managing it'. Behaviours of isolation then begin including keeping an eye on the victims, managing their hours and frequent collection of money, they then isolate them further and is followed by acts of intimidation (Verhoeven et al, 2015). By now you may have noticed that although domestic abuse forms a large proportion of police work, many of the commonly cited causes of repeat victimisation are shared with other crime types. In your practice, if you are able to provide an intervention that helps to break this cycle you can help protect victims from serious ongoing harm.

VICTIMOLOGY

Victimology is the study of the victim's interaction with crime and whether that has a bearing on their status as a victim. Victimology is much more theoretical than the other areas already discussed. But by understanding the theory you might be able to see it in action with those whom you interact with and allow it to challenge your thoughts and equally create suitable interventions to help prevent harm.

POSITIVIST VICTIMOLOGY

Positivism believes that through scientific endeavour and investigation you can link behaviour and factors to the result – crime. Proponents believe that, rather than offender-centric theories whereby factors influence offender behaviour, factors and circumstances influence how a victim became victimised (Dignan, 2005). Vonhentig (1940) argued that while there are some crimes that have no direct involvement of the victim, there are frequent occasions where a victim consents, co-operates, conspires or provokes the offence into taking place. In essence, his work states victims contribute to their own victimisation by contributing to or fostering a situation where they are likely to be victimised (Fattah, 2000).

There are, understandably, some obvious criticisms to this. First, it attempts to normalise and accept victim blaming. The common version of such an argument in this matter is that 'she was raped because of the clothing she was wearing'. While some may argue that a victim's clothing was a factor in the offender's acts, this is entirely unacceptable thinking and ultimately has nothing to do with the suspect's decision to rape. It also assumes that a victim's identity is obvious; however, for state-based crime this is not the case. How can it be argued that the state caused someone to drink drive?

CRITICAL VICTIMOLOGY

Critical victimology looks at the concept of being a victim more broadly and questions who has the power to define someone as a victim. Sandra Walklate (1990) in her article utilises two examples to highlight this argument. The first relates to a gas leak, which took place in Bhopal, India in 1984. This resulted in mass fatalities with estimates ranging from 1754 to 5000 people; in addition, estimates have suggested that an additional two people die every week since the accident due to the exposure to the gas. Despite that, however, the Indian government only acknowledged 3329 deaths for compensation purposes. Additionally, she argued that the pesticide plant that was subject to the leak was not profitable for a time before and that information was used by the experts to determine and frame the material reality of the people that work there when they were awarded compensation.

A common criticism with this viewpoint on victimology is the historically ignored crimes, for example, domestic violence. There is never an argument that these victims were not victims. Equally, even despite not being in a public discourse, the nature of them being victims was not discounted.

RESTORATIVE JUSTICE

Restorative justice (RJ) is briefly discussed in Chapter 4 of another book in this series, *Police Procedure and Evidence in the Criminal Justice System* (Archer et al, 2023). It is a relatively new practice within the CJS in England and Wales. It is defined as a process through which parties who have some involvement in the offence collectively resolve how to deal with the aftermath of the offence and its implications (CPS, 2019).

RJ is seen to put the victim's perspective into view and works on what can be done to repair harm in a CJS, which is often offender-centric. It does not work on the theory that the victim is always right, an example being a victim could be overly vindictive to the criminal. But what it does do is listen to everyone involved and works on not only the suspect but also transforming victims' attitudes towards offenders. This could, for example, mean that the victim is more understanding or supportive when community sentences are given to an offender that will benefit from having heard their story (Bennett, 2007).

The Association of Chief Police Officers (ACPO) now the National Police Chiefs Council (NPCC) set three levels of RJ, which will guide you as to the best approach to give dependent on the situation.

1. Level 1 – informal RJ: this often takes place on the street where police officers resolve low-level crime or anti-social behaviour. This can be accommodated via a community resolution and hopes to diffuse a situation immediately.

2. Level 2 – RJ can be used instead of or alongside the formal criminal justice process. It can be organised by officers or staff either for when level 1 RJ could not take place or for more serious offences.

3. Level 3 – this is for complex and sensitive cases where the offenders should be monitored and should be conducted by experienced RJ facilitators. These can be pre- or post-sentence and in prison if required (College of Policing, 2022b).

These three levels show that regardless of the offence type, RJ is an option; however, based on the circumstances, the approach to RJ will have to alter accordingly.

EVIDENCE-BASED POLICING

In New Zealand 'Project Restore' is a 'survivor-driven' organisation offering restorative conferences in cases of sexual violence. It aims to support the offender in understanding the actions of the behaviour and develop an action plan with them, which could include reparation to the victim but also therapeutic programmes.

At the time of its review, 29 referrals had been received of which nine had resulted in case conferences. This high attrition rate was due to the high threshold to managing risk and the readiness of all those involved.

Of those taking part in the research, both victims and offenders expressed satisfaction with the process. The victim reported gaining strength from the process and clarity about what happened (McGlynn et al, 2012).

> This example shows that regardless of the offence type, RJ can be conducted subject to all parties being appropriate. It also shows its value in helping both the victim and suspect to move on and understand what took place and the effects it has had on them.

HOW CAN THIS HELP ME LOOK AFTER VICTIMS?

The CJS can be cold. Often courts are seen as overbearing and often direct when it comes to discussing the facts but despite that, victims should remain at the centre of it. Without them there would be no CJS and as you are aware we police by consent. By understanding common victim vulnerabilities or how people become entrapped within an abusive relationship not only do you improve your practice but when you present a case to the CPS or a decision maker you are able to do so with the understanding and arguments needed should they be less understanding. While you may not know how someone got into that position, you can at least address them with some level of understanding, hopefully increasing both victim confidence and, more importantly, your ability to safeguard them. In interviewing, rapport is vital and, in some cases, can be the only way you can ensure justice comes through, so think about as a victim how much easier it will be to speak to the police if they at least have some knowledge of what they are going through.

Crime recording is perhaps a harder area to understand its impact on victims but to do so you need to look at the political landscape policing operates in. Would victims rather have a properly funded and resourced police service that meets their needs or one that maintains the status quo? You can see from the earlier discussion about crime recording standards that the government can use them to monitor certain MOs and the media use them to hold the government and the service to account. This may not immediately assist victims, but by understanding the reasoning and the rules, longer term you will improve the services received by victims.

Finally, at the start of this section, the CJS was described as cold. RJ, while fitting somewhat outside the system, does play a role in making the victim feel part of the process and less victimised by the CJS itself. You can see parts of RJ in victim impact statements but think about why you first became or wanted to become an officer. Many will probably mention making a difference to victims and RJ has been shown to help victims recover and suspects address their offending behaviour and as such should not be sidelined in favour of criminal convictions.

SUMMARY OF KEY CONCEPTS

This chapter has examined a range of factors involving crime statistics and victims.

- Crime can be measured in a number of ways. The main two in England and Wales are police recorded crime and the CSEW.

- The CSEW was established to address the 'dark figure of crime'. This is the idea that not all offences are recorded by the police and as such were missing from previous statistics.

- Repeat victims have a range of vulnerabilities and their repeat victimisation could be a show of their trauma response to the incident.

- Victimology looks at how the victim interacts with the crime and in part its causation.

- Positivist victimology links the commission of the crime to the victim and attempts to do so through a scientific-like examination.

- Critical victimology argues that the status of the victim is defined by those in power.

- RJ seeks to made amends for the damage caused by the crime and links the victim and offender together with the aim of having a meaningful conversation.

CHECK YOUR KNOWLEDGE

1. Why does police recorded crime differ so much to the crime survey?

2. Explain how a trauma response to crime might explain why people are repeatedly victimised?

3. What characteristics of the victim have been linked to increased chances of becoming a victim of crime?

4. What does 'event dependency' mean when it comes to being a repeat victim of crime?

5. What are the different levels of RJ intervention?

Sample answers are provided at the end of this book.

FURTHER READING

Dignan, J (2005) *Understanding Victims and Restorative Justice.* Maidenhead: Open University Press.
This book provides an accessible read to the topics covered in this chapter and is aimed to allow students to understand the wider issues in victim-based issues and RJ. If you wish to read further or want to get a deeper understanding, I strongly recommend this book.

Fattah, E A (2000) Victimology: Past, Present and Future. *Criminologie*, 33(1): 17–46.
This journal article is translated from French; however, it provides a much more academic look at victimology and presents the arguments both for and against each approach well and does so in a manner that is not obstructively academic. If as part of your studies you need to write about victimology, this article is a great place to start.

Home Office (2022) *Home Office Counting Rules 2022/3.* London: Home Office.
I do not suggest you read all of this document as it is very lengthy and will not help you instantly become a good officer. However, a reasonable working knowledge of the HOCR will be beneficial in your practice especially if your force requires you to classify the crimes yourself. Equally, crime recording at the time of writing is a favoured area of scrutiny on forces by the HMICFRS. As a result, minimal mistakes will be beneficial to both you and your force.

CHAPTER 2
OFFENDERS AND THE CAUSES OF OFFENDING

LEARNING OBJECTIVES

AFTER READING THIS CHAPTER YOU WILL BE ABLE TO:

- understand offenders' risks and vulnerabilities and why people turn to criminal careers;

- explain a range of different criminological theories behind why people offend and contrast them with each other;

- reflect on how this knowledge can impact your policing style;

- recognise potential ways of identifying offenders.

INTRODUCTION

Offenders are always the subject of media interest, whether that be the news, movies, podcasts or TV shows, and if you look at programmes such as *Criminal Minds* pretty much the whole programme is dedicated to understanding the offender (although please do not base your entire practice in policing upon the show). While some people think that policing should just concentrate on catching bad guys, understanding them is crucial in this. When you do catch criminals, you also need to understand what to do next. Despite what some people think, you do not always just send people to court and there is an increasing use of out-of-court disposals. To understand which disposal option is the best choice to prevent re-offending and impact on the victim you must understand the offender. This chapter equips you to understand the issues involved in this process.

WHO OFFENDS?

Understandably, there is no single 'typical' offender. However, looking at the statistics of convicted offenders (please remember, however, not all offenders are caught) you can start to form an image of a core group of offenders. For example, looking at convicted sex offenders, many of them were male, white and on the whole had not been previously cautioned or convicted for sexual offences (Office for National Statistics, 2013). This does not mean you should be rounding up everyone who fits these categories whenever a new offence takes place, but it does mean that we need to be creative when looking for offenders and a crime database search may not help us locate them.

THE AGE-OFFENDING CURVE

Criminologists have tried to address the question of who commits crime for some time and one model created is the age–offending curve, which relates to increased prevalence of offending at certain ages rather than number of offences committed. This model argues that criminality increases from the age someone obtains criminal responsibility and reaches its peak in the teenage years. Having reached its peak, it then declines initially rapidly; however, as time goes on, this decline slows (Farrington, 1986).

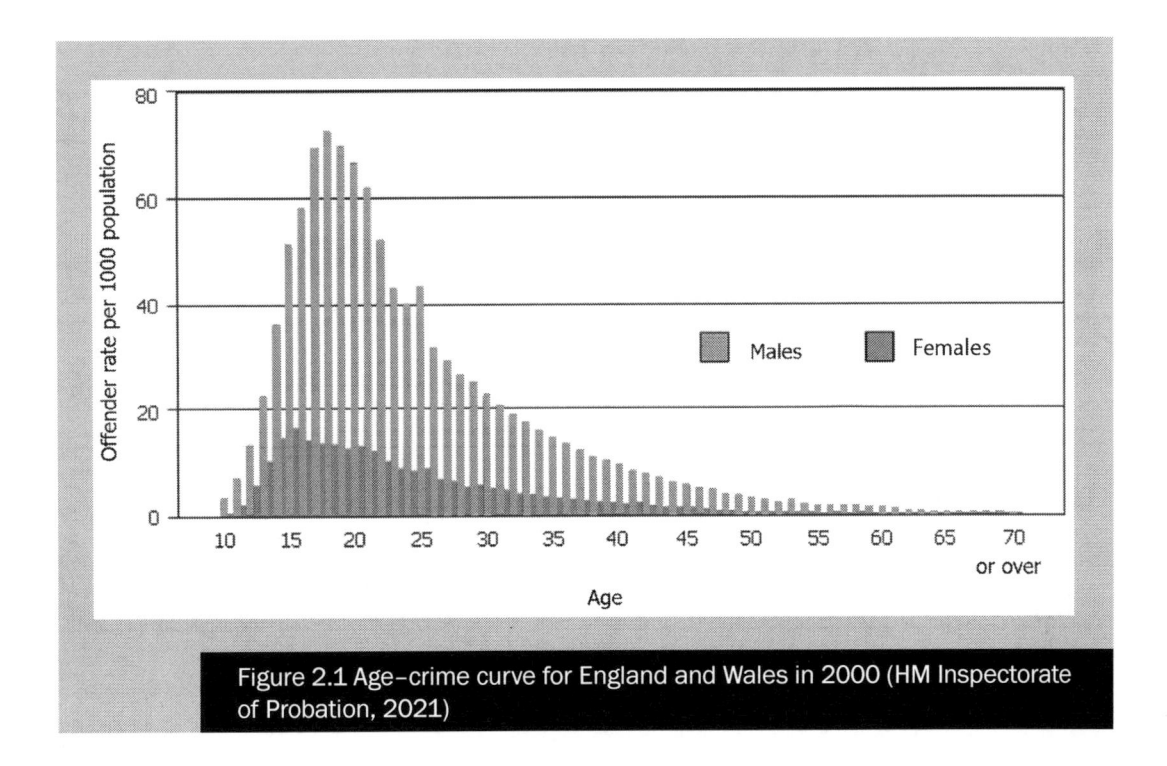

Figure 2.1 Age–crime curve for England and Wales in 2000 (HM Inspectorate of Probation, 2021)

As you can see from Figure 2.1, this model created in 1986 is still relevant today, with offenders in 2000 still fitting in mostly with the described curve.

As with any sort of theory or model it is not perfect, and a key criticism comes in relation to its modelling of offending as the data used to create it was entirely from prosecution data and not self-reporting and therefore fails to consider the dark figure of crime (see Chapter 1). It could also be argued that the increased prevalence at a younger age is due to offenders still learning their craft and therefore they are more likely to be caught. The rapid decline might tie in with this – skill comes with practise, so offenders are just not being caught as much once they have finessed their craft.

During your studies you may have come across the idea of the 'revolving door of offending', which comes from research that has shown that if people have previously offended, the likelihood of them re-offending is increased. Research has also used offenders' previous offence type to provide a statistical likelihood of their next offence. For example, one study (Wolfgang et al, 1972) has shown that for an injury offence there is a probability of 0.5 that the next arrest would be for a minor offence. (For those not keen on mathematics, if something has a probability of one it is certain to happen; if it has a probability of zero then it will not happen; the higher the number between these shows an increased probability of it happening.) There are, however, some causal links. For example, if you were arrested for theft, the likelihood of you being arrested again for theft was 0.271; if, however, you were arrested for assault, the likelihood of you being arrested for theft in the future was only 0.128. It has also been shown that offenders demonstrate a broad range of offending rather than specialising in a particular area (Smith, 2007).

CRITICAL THINKING ACTIVITY 2.1

LEVEL 4

- Research offenders for a crime type of your choosing.

- Review the current statistics for convicted offenders and formulate a picture of a 'typical' offender.

- Try to explain why that profile might be the case – why does that crime type lend itself to a certain type of people (or no particular group at all)?

- Is there any research apart from convictions that would indicate a different section of society?

- If so, why might that be?

- Using this information, is there anything you can think of that could be done to help change that picture?

COMMON DISADVANTAGES OFFENDERS EXPERIENCE

Before exploring a range of theories around offenders and why they may offend, it is important to look at common issues offenders have reported experiencing prior to offending. When it comes to community policing, your influence in these areas might impact on criminal commissioning rates in the future. For example, a Home Office report (Budd et al, 2005) looked at self-reported offenders and highlighted some common areas.

- Early exit from full-time education – those that left prior to the age of 15 were most likely to commit an offence. While there was no clear relationship between level of education and offending history, those with post-secondary school academic qualifications were least likely to offend.

- Having been in care – those in local authority care, sometimes referred to as LAC (looked after child), are more likely to have committed offences than others.

- Unstable accommodation – those in stable accommodation were least likely to commit an offence; those who were not were most likely to take part in acquisitive crime. These two might have a mutually reinforcing relationship.

- Alcohol use – this is a more complex relationship depending on the offence type, but regular drinkers were more likely to be involved in violent crime. However, for theft offences, infrequent and non-drinkers were just as likely to offend.

- Drug use – theft offences were strongly associated with drug use; however, criminal damage and violence less so; 86 per cent of prisoners surveyed in this study reported drug use.

The first two bullet points relate to an increasingly researched area of ACEs. These are defined as stressful or traumatic events, which if you have witnessed growing up put you at an increased risk of health issues, early death and risk of crime. A study in a Welsh prison in 2018 found that over eight out of 10 prisoners reported at least one ACE and nearly half had four or more (Ford et al, 2019). The Centre for Disease Control and Prevention (Freeze, 2019) has identified 10 different types of experience, which if an individual is exposed to prior to the age of 18 impacts on their future:

1. *emotional abuse;*

2. *physical abuse;*

3. *sexual abuse;*

4. *emotional neglect;*

5. *physical neglect;*

6. *domestic violence towards their mother;*

7. household substance use;

8. household mental illness;

9. parental separation;

10. household member with prison history.

(Wolff and Baglivio, 2016, p 8)

While an entire chapter could be dedicated to the increasingly researched area of ACEs and criminality, it is useful to understand that identification of the above issues and early intervention could help with prevention in the long term. You can find more information on ACEs in Chapters 1 and 3 of *Policing Mental Health, Vulnerability and Risk* also in this series (Williams, 2023).

The next most common issue was drug and substance misuse. Research has shown that typically these people offend to fund their habit and as such most offenders with an addiction are linked to low-level acquisitive crime rather than more serious violent offences such as robbery (Pierce et al, 2015). Research by McMurran (2007) argued that drug treatment programmes in prisons were not as effective as cognitive behavioural therapy (CBT) programmes or therapeutic communities where people are held to account by each other for their behaviours while given support.

While it might be quite easy to label an offender by the offences they present to you at the time, often these are due to a web of complex issues. A longer-term solution to crime could be to address these.

POLICING SPOTLIGHT

One example of where ACEs can be seen in an offender is the case of Ava White. She was aged 12 and was stabbed to death by a boy aged 15 following a dispute on Snapchat. Media reports following the murder described him as grinning having stabbed Ava in the neck before fleeing the scene.

Interestingly, in regard to ACEs, the boy, who cannot be named, was described as having ADHD (attention deficit hyperactivity disorder), attended a special school, was suspected as being exploited by criminals and had witnessed domestic abuse against his mother in 2015 (BBC News, 2022). While the full details of what built up to his offending will not be known publicly, it is an example of ACEs' prevalence in offenders.

CRITICAL THINKING ACTIVITY 2.2

LEVEL 4

Consider ACEs and substance and/or alcohol misuse.

- What options does policing have to positively influence people's lives regarding these factors?

ACEs are not typical policing matters and the children at the time of experiencing them are not criminals. Consider the pros and cons to policing engaging in this area.

- Do you think these issues are better suited for other agencies to deal with and, if so, who and what can they offer?

Sample answers are provided at the end of this book.

REFLECTIVE PRACTICE 2.1

LEVEL 4

Look on any police force's social media account at a post where the force has shown a conviction of an offender and review the comments. Sexual offenders usually provide good case studies.

- Based on what is written, what is your impression of the offender?

- How many people categorise the offender on the offence type?

- Does anyone stand up for the offender or provide background to their offending?

- Based on the information on the post and the attached police article, if there is one, formulate a profile for the offender.

- If you were to re-write the post, what information could you include to improve the discussion about the offender?

BIOLOGICAL REASONS FOR OFFENDING

LOMBROSO

One of the more famous biological reasons for people offending was written by Lombroso. He graduated in 1858 and unsurprisingly his background was biology, and his doctoral thesis was about 'cretinism and pellagra'. He then worked in the military where he began studying soldiers and examining the differences in them according to the various regions in Italy (Wolfgang, 1961). This led him into his first steps of his criminological career with his first version of the book *Criminal Man*, which argued that there were biological reasons for people offending. He believed that offenders did so due to them being '*atavistic and degenerate heredity of the born criminal*' (Ellwood, 1912, p 717).

He described criminals as sub-human and states that they are:

> *Reproductions of not only savage men but also the most ferocious carnivores and rodents. This discovery should not make us more compassionate towards born criminals but rather should shield us from pity, for these beasts are members not of our species.*
>
> (Lombroso, 2006, p 348)

Lombroso examined a range of factors for offending. In his first book, the first chapter reviews 66 different skull types and shows how cranial development indicates how some people are of lower development and mark specific groups. He also reviewed tattoos and provided an insight into the placement and meaning. As time went on and in subsequent versions of *Criminal Man*, Lombroso started to incorporate psychological and sociological reasons for offending. However, he still cited that the main driver was biology; in his later work, for example, he does a palm analysis of criminal men, 'normal men' and monkeys (Delisi, 2013).

A number of major criticisms of this theory were established shortly after its publication. First, it is widely rejected by the medical profession, and religious leaders at the time did not approve of it due to the abandonment of 'moral responsibility' (Rock, 2007). If this theory is correct – and it is widely disputed – it is important to ask whether a biological urge makes people offend or if their biology just makes them more susceptible to offend. If it is the first option, the idea of *mens rea*, the guilty mind, a key element in proving most offences, becomes obsolete implying these individuals have no control at all. Let us also think about all the rehabilitative work with offenders. If biology were a key factor, how would this work have any impact on re-offending?

It is clear from more up-to-date research that this theory is questionable. That said, it is important to know such theories do exist, to understand how social science has evolved and be able to challenge such opinions of criminals.

CRITICAL THINKING ACTIVITY 2.3

LEVEL 5

- Considering Lombroso's theory, what would be the impact if we were to use it in modern day policing?

- Are there any benefits to doing so?

- What are the dangers?

SOCIOLOGICAL THEORIES OF OFFENDING

There are a broad range of sociological theories that attempt to explain why people offend. For the purposes of this book, I have selected the two that are likely to have the most impact on your practice.

BROKEN WINDOWS THEORY

Broken windows theory was developed following an experiment by American psychologist, Philip Zimbardo (1970). He left two vehicles unattended without licence plates, one in the Bronx, New York and the other in California. He observed that within 10 minutes the car in the Bronx was attacked and had bits removed whereas the car in California remained untouched for about a week. After that week, however, he smashed a window and consequently within hours the car had been nearly destroyed. The explanation given for this bases itself around people caring. In the Bronx, people walk around with anonymity and cars were broken into frequently and as such when they see a car with a little bit of damage, they associate it with a lack of care. In California, further damage only took place when the social acceptance of no one caring for that vehicle was reached. This type of act has also been recreated on a low level in one study within a university by leaving a common room a mess; when the researcher did so the likelihood of littering increased from 26 per cent to 45 per cent (Ramos and Torgler, 2012).

When it comes to more serious offences it is argued that when visible signs of disorder go unchallenged it is likely to breed further disorder as people feel there is no challenge to that behaviour. As a result, Wilson and Kelling (1982), who were the first to coin the phrase 'broken windows' in their subsequent article on the original study, argue that by targeting minor offences you could reduce more serious crime (Newburn, 2007, p 575).

POLICING SPOTLIGHT

An example of broken windows theory in action can be seen in Grimsby in 2022. The council here issued 38 homes with legal notices within the East Marsh area following almost a third of fly-tipping reports from Grimsby coming from that one area.

The council attended the area, cleaned it up and then issued legal notices to homes, on the premise that if the area were in a better condition, it would be looked after by the residents. The council helped addresses that often left rubbish in the street and then utilised enforcement if required.

The project itself did not produce the reduction the council was hoping for in fly tipping but did allow them to identify problem addresses and deal with them to prevent further issues (Sloper, 2022) and therefore was a partial success for seeing broken windows theory in action.

Broken windows theory is therefore about signs and signals of care. You might find during your own practice there are areas that are more rundown to which you are called more often. You should consider whether this is broken windows theory in action.

The theory is not without its issues. It is based around anecdotal evidence. When one study tried to enact broken windows policing in New York it found that crime rates went up (Harcourt and Ludwig, 2006). This could be explained utilising the discussion in the previous chapter regarding crime recording and the dark figure of crime and it could be because the police were paying more attention to those offences and consequently recording them when previously they may not have done so.

Another paper by Konkel et al (2019) argues that it may not be the number of crimes or disorder that matter when it comes to broken windows theory but it is the signals of disorder that are important. They argue that it is likely that levels of disorder will be continuous but also unseen. It is those issues that show to people and offenders lack of care, which may remove the inhibition of others to offend. The same study also saw a link to suggest that minor offences are indicative of more serious offences taking place and that community-oriented policing is a good method to preventing neighbourhood decline (Konkel et al, 2019).

LABELLING THEORY

Another sociological theory is labelling theory, which centres around the proposition that the official labelling of behaviour as deviant becomes self-fulling for offenders. Becker argued that criminality is caused by external judgements or labels on an individual. This then negatively impacts on their self-perception and as such pushes them towards offending. It is argued as a response of this theory we can see the rise of community mental health, decriminalisation of behaviour and diversion schemes (Petrunik, 1980).

POLICING SPOTLIGHT

A man has been sentenced for a cruel campaign of stalking against a number of individuals who innocently went dog walking in New Street Park during which time he would follow them home, send them abusive letters and leave dog excrement on their cars wherever they went.

These incidents took place over the course of two years and 32-year-old Scott, based near to the park, has been convicted and has been given a community order because of these offences.

CRITICAL THINKING ACTIVITY 2.4

LEVEL 4

- Consider the judgement placed upon the offender and how someone might see them in public knowing the information published. Explain your thoughts.

- Do you think this post encourages individuals to rehabilitate or encourages the public to see offenders as bad people?

Labelling theory also highlights issues with various types of offenders. For example, when it comes to sexual offenders, we have seen 'name and shame' campaigns in the media, which often encourage public anger and sometimes vigilante action, which as a result leads to isolation from the law-abiding community and as a consequence leads to re-offending (McAlinden, 2005).

There are some issues with this theory. For example, it argues that labelling acts as deviant makes them bad. However, it could be argued that some acts are intrinsically bad regardless of whether they have been labelled so or not. As an example, if you were to kill your partner's cat, regardless of whether you thought it was bad at the time of the act, I would suggest that act is still fundamentally bad and frowned upon.

Secondly, there is a similar argument for those acts that have been labelled as criminal by law but others that are subject to debate. Think about the amount of resistance faced by people who still use their mobile phones while driving. Does committing a traffic offence make you a bad person?

Finally, this theory indicates that the act of being caught is what makes people enter criminal careers; however, not all criminals get caught. Does that mean that these criminals do not do bad things? Or does it mean that members of the community do not think they are bad?

In practice, however, there is value in this theory especially regarding young people in 'the system' – these people classified as 'bad' meaning they are consequently treated as such by both policing and other agencies. As seen in the research about sexual offenders, this can lead them to be marginalised and feel like there is little option but to re-offend.

REFLECTIVE PRACTICE 2.2

LEVEL 5

- Imagine a time in your policing career when you have met or come across an individual that was labelled as 'bad' or 'troublesome'. What could you do to challenge that opinion?

- Put yourself in the shoes of that individual. What do you think your experiences would be with authority having achieved the label of 'bad'?

- Is there anything you could do to help build bridges with this individual? What would the benefits be of doing so?

PSYCHOLOGICAL REASONS FOR OFFENDING

When it comes to psychological theories of offending there are two key theories that I think will assist in your policing practice: rational choice theory and routine activity theory.

RATIONAL CHOICE THEORY

Rational choice theory argues that people make decisions based on the incentives and constraints that affect their behaviour. Imagine the idea of the offender's mind as a set of weighing scales with a pros and cons list on either side – if there are more positives than negatives it is a worthwhile endeavour to go out and offend. A basic example can be seen in Figure 2.2, which considers potential pros and cons of a burglar reviewing an address.

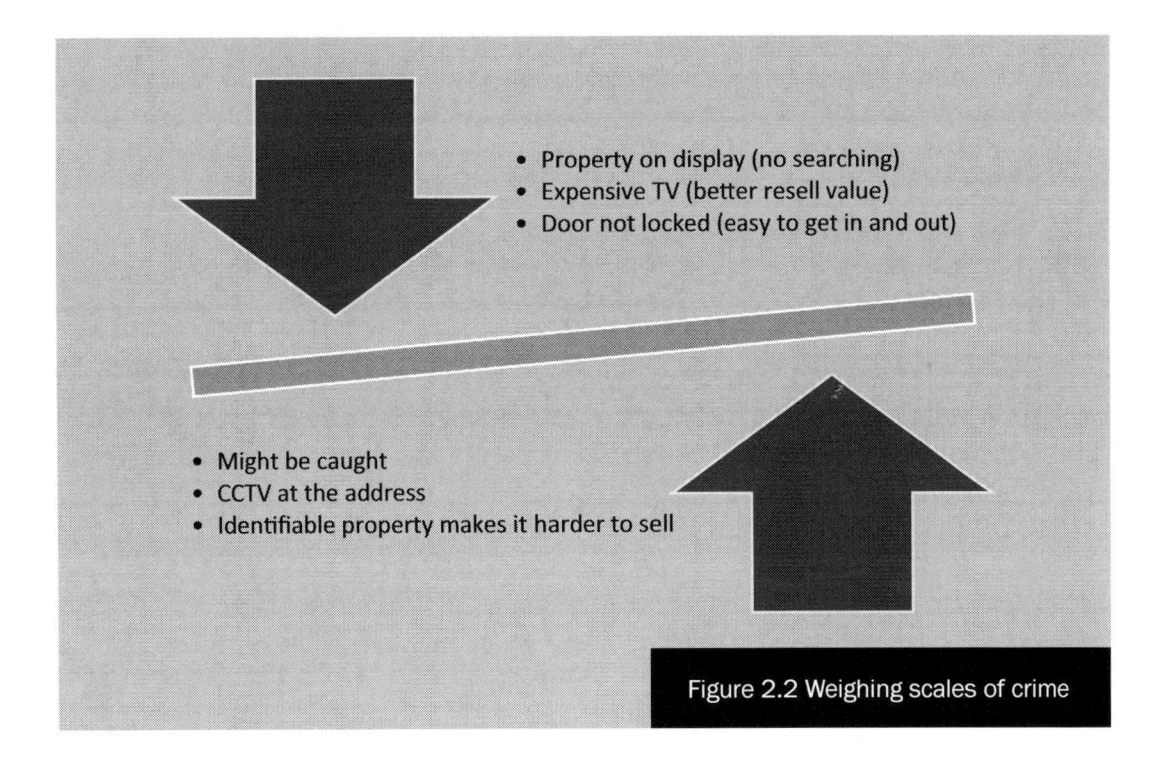

- Property on display (no searching)
- Expensive TV (better resell value)
- Door not locked (easy to get in and out)

- Might be caught
- CCTV at the address
- Identifiable property makes it harder to sell

Figure 2.2 Weighing scales of crime

As with all theories, rational choice theory has evolved and now consists of a number of key principles including general deterrence and specific deterrence. As theorists expanded the theory it then included incapacitation and retributive justice theory and 'just deserts' (Keel, 2019).

General deterrence is the idea that people will engage in criminal and deviant activities if they do not fear apprehension and punishment. This means that if people do not fear being captured because there is no police or security to enforce it, and even if they do get caught the punishment is minimal, why would they not take the risk? Think back to when you last played Monopoly – inevitably someone took that extra note at some point (unless you have the fancy digital version) but why? It is just a game but the reward of winning compared with the cost of getting caught and the punishment for being caught makes it worthwhile. If we translate it to crime, what do you think the purpose of all those signs up in your local supermarket saying 'shoplifters will be prosecuted' are for? Surely it is obvious that there is CCTV and shoplifters will be prosecuted but, by having signs present, they are increasing the fear of capture.

EVIDENCE-BASED POLICING

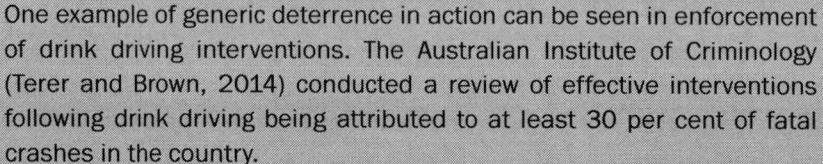

One example of generic deterrence in action can be seen in enforcement of drink driving interventions. The Australian Institute of Criminology (Terer and Brown, 2014) conducted a review of effective interventions following drink driving being attributed to at least 30 per cent of fatal crashes in the country.

In Australia, random breath testing takes place and it does so with the aim of deterring people from drink driving, rather than catching those that have. They found that general deterrence took place when drivers' awareness of breath testing was increased. However, for it to be effective, the deterrence should be sustained so that awareness remains in the public memory.

The same paper also cites that following the introduction of random breath testing in Finland there was a reduction of 58 per cent in drink driving.

This clearly shows that, at least in relation to drink driving, general deterrence works to prevent offending.

Specific deterrence focuses much more on the individual and their future behaviours. This is where known criminals are targeted thus preventing them from becoming future criminals and breaching the social norms. Think about a crime type that policing focuses heavily on to minimise risk, such as domestic violence. Many forces have a positive action policy and while this does not necessarily impact on the criminal justice outcome it could be argued that it impacts on the individuals' decisions to commit such an offence in the first place.

Incapacitation relies on the idea that the punishment should be effective. If we look at England and Wales statistics, a House of Lords report (Blakey, 2017) states that 49.2 per cent of offenders re-offend within a year of being released or if they are sentenced to a year or less in prison this increases to 65.5 per cent. With those statistics it can be argued that the purpose of imprisonment is not to rehabilitate but to prevent them from offending again by locking them inside. The rational choice element to this is that if deterrence has failed what other course can you follow other than to lock them up?

Retributive justice means that a subjectively appropriate punishment should be given to people who have broken the law. This can be achieved in a number of ways whether that be through cost, loss or suffering, the latter of which can be both material and symbolic (Wenzel and Okimoto, 2016). That means if you were to be blinded following an assault, the punishment should reflect such hurt, albeit I do not recommend the removal of an eye as part of a conditional caution. If we put ourselves in the shoes of the offender, it would certainly dissuade them from offending again.

POLICING SPOTLIGHT

Consider the weighing scales for someone who is subjected to child criminal exploitation in the drug market. Bobby is 14 years old, has low attainment at school and is frequently in trouble meaning he has a poor relationship with staff. His parents have a low income and struggle with reading and writing and as such do not get all the support they need as they are unable to do the paperwork. Financially, this means that they only have one or two meals a day.

Bobby's benefits from engaging in the drug market are that he receives gifts including expensive shoes and money, and he no longer must go to school, is fed three meals a day and has increased status with his peers as they are seeking access to the drugs he sells. The negatives, however, are he has now lost control of his life, he used to be allowed to roam the streets without punishment, but now that is no longer the case, and he is often taken to unfamiliar areas. As a result of the business model of the drug supply he is at risk of physical assaults should something go wrong, which in the past has included a broken nose after he himself was robbed.

REFLECTIVE PRACTICE 2.3

LEVEL 4

- Given the above circumstances consider how you could interact or deal with the individual to mitigate these pull factors towards offending and maximise the push factors away from offending.

- Is there any other agency you might want to get involved?

Before moving on to the next theory, it is worth highlighting that this theory is not without criticism. For example, it tends to focus on individuals' behaviour: what about those who operate in gangs or offend as part of a wider group such as young people who offend to further their relationships and sense of belonging (Weaver and Fraser, 2022)? In a similar vein, it assumes that people want to maximise their own goals and are self-interested (Gul, 2009). If we consider the reasons why you joined policing, it is certainly not for gain or the huge wage; why does offending have to be any different?

ROUTINE ACTIVITY THEORY

The second theory this section considers is routine activity theory. This was originally coined by Cohen and Felson in 1979 who were researching the rise in crime following the Second World War. They theorise that changes in the patterns of daily activity mean that would-be offenders have now increasingly got more suitable targets with a lack of suitable guardians, which previously was not the case. Their argument was that usual measures that would signal increases in crime such as poverty had improved but crime had worsened. What had changed at the time was people's daily activities such as working. One example they cite was the increase of women working meaning homes were left unattended and women themselves were now exposed to more offenders in the public arena (Miro, 2014).

Routine activity theory therefore argues that just like the fire triangle, crime must have three key components, which if converging at the same time and location lead to an offence taking place (Figure 2.3).

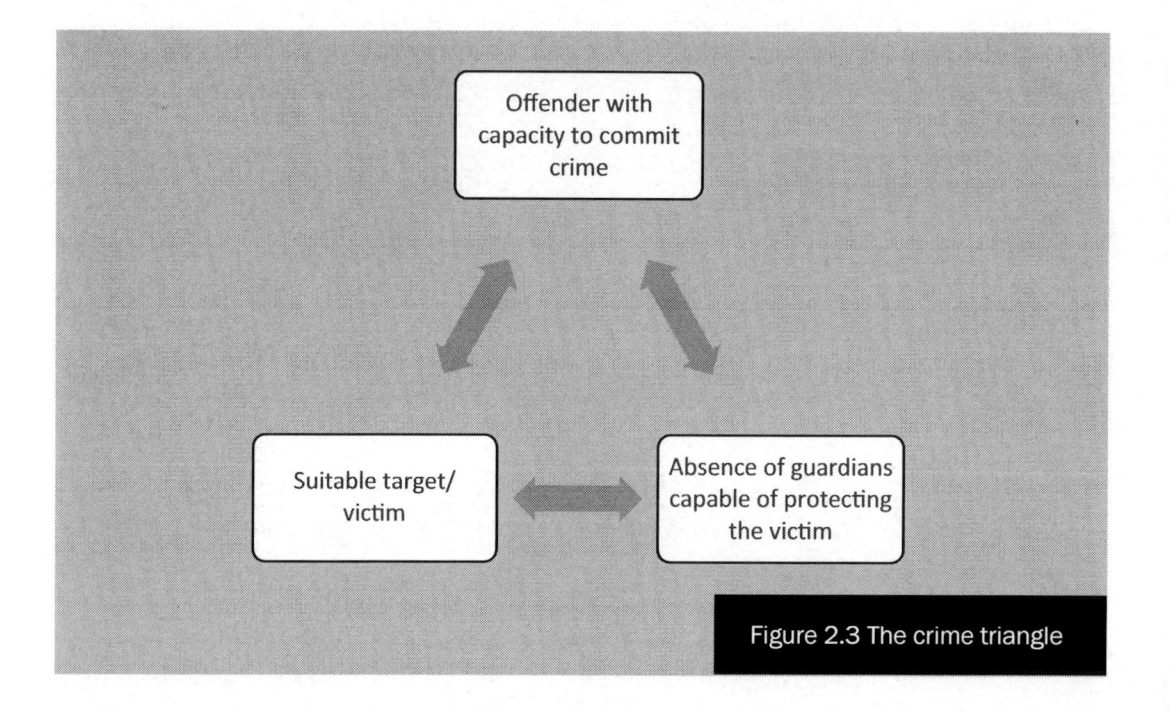

Figure 2.3 The crime triangle

POLICING SPOTLIGHT

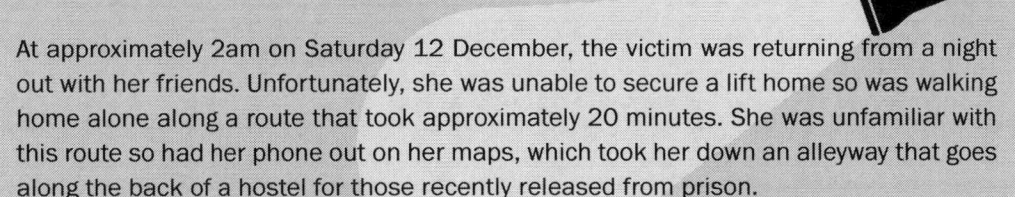

At approximately 2am on Saturday 12 December, the victim was returning from a night out with her friends. Unfortunately, she was unable to secure a lift home so was walking home alone along a route that took approximately 20 minutes. She was unfamiliar with this route so had her phone out on her maps, which took her down an alleyway that goes along the back of a hostel for those recently released from prison.

The victim did not see her attacker as the alleyway was dark but on hearing them coming with nowhere else to run, she decided to scream. No one heard her due to the alleyway being situated between residential properties and a play park. On the residential side, which is the same side as the hostel, the addresses had overgrown plants so people from the park and alleyway cannot see into the addresses and the occupants were used to the sounds of children using their mopeds illegally on the footpath and park area.

The offender, who was a man, should have been on tag with a curfew between the hours of 7pm and 7am, which is GPS monitored; however, this had not been fitted yet. To assist, the hostel offered to check that the man was abiding by his conditions. This hostel used to be staffed at nights but due to cutbacks was only staffed between the hours of 7am and 10pm. Owing to previous issues in the hostel, it had CCTV; however, it was poor quality in the dark and there were no cameras outside.

CRITICAL THINKING ACTIVITY 2.5

LEVEL 4

- How can you use Figure 2.3 to help prevent offences from taking place utilising a rape scenario?

- In the Policing Spotlight above what factors can be altered to potentially prevent an offence from taking place?

While routine activity theory can be used in a practical sense, it is still important to highlight potential pitfalls in the theory. When it was written, it heavily focused on location-based crimes and its sole argument is that all three must converge in one location. However, increasingly with the rise of online crime this is not the case. Proponents of the theory suggest it is the same principles applied to these offences but rather than the factors meeting in the physical space they do so in the digital space. For example, the lack of a suitable guardian could be incorrectly updated anti-virus protection (Reynes, 2013).

ENVIRONMENTAL CRIMINOLOGY

Environmental criminology argues that the environment where the crime takes place and the offenders' interactions with it influence the reasons why the offenders offend. The Chicago School were key proponents of this theory and their theory alongside distance decay theory are explained below.

THE CHICAGO SCHOOL

One example of environmental impact on crime, which was created by the Chicago School, was written by Park et al (1925). They spent large amounts of time studying Chicago and consequently managed to break down the city into five concentric circles portraying environmental zones (Figure 2.4).

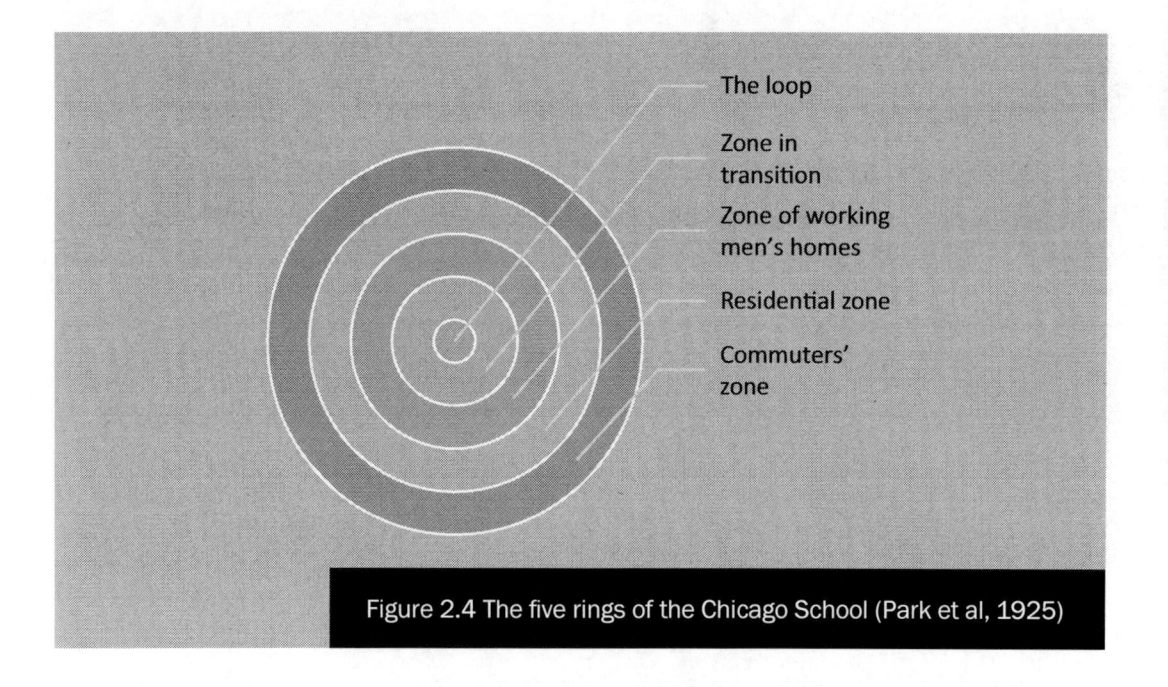

Figure 2.4 The five rings of the Chicago School (Park et al, 1925)

- The loop
- Zone in transition
- Zone of working men's homes
- Residential zone
- Commuters' zone

These separate zones or districts had different functions within the city and naturally attracted different forms of crime. The loop was the central business district zone and tends to house key businesses as well as shopping. The zone of transition is an industrial area where change is taking place at pace; this also therefore tends to be the area that had the 'slum or semi-slums'. The zone of working men's homes is for working men as it has proximity to the factory area and as such its key attraction is its accessibility. The residential zone houses the middle class and finally the commuter zone is the suburban areas.

In regard to crime, therefore, the areas that typically attracted criminals were spaces where ethnic cultures collided such as the zone of transition. Here housing was more run down and there was a great prevalence of poverty (Carrabine et al, 2009). Area type also indicates what type of offences take place; for example, the central business district will typically have more white-collar crimes and the residential zones will have more burglaries. We can see echoes of this theory in modern policing within London. While there is no perfect ringed model, if you look at the City of London it is a square mile that is seen as the financial hub of the city, and it is in a central location. Consequently, its unique police force not only undertake all the usual functions of policing but also are the national lead on fraud and cybercrime, given that traditionally this impacted those within that area more.

As with all theories, this one is not without criticism. This theory tells us where criminals generally live but not always where the crimes occur, which means when applying this theory to crime prevention, its impact can be minimal. In addition, different types of crime generally have a very different spatial patterning; for example, assaults would be expected to be seen more around bars and clubs whereas burglaries would typically be within residential areas (Brantingham and Brantingham, 1975). This, however, does not require a model and can be seen as more common sense and practicality. Finally, while the model itself may have been effective at modelling cities it can be argued it does not accurately reflect cities today, many of which have been subject to regeneration and urban sprawl. We can see on a basic level with the rise of out-of-town shopping centres how zones of development do not apply to urban areas today.

REFLECTIVE PRACTICE 2.4

LEVEL 4

- Consider the area you police or your hometown. Can you identify these separate areas as shown above?

- Knowing these different areas and what crime would typically take place there, how can you alter your patrolling accordingly?

DISTANCE DECAY THEORY

The second theory is distance decay theory. This geographical theory still supports the idea of free will and individuality of offenders. However, it argues that offenders act within a framework of geographic constraints, a major factor of which is distance. This means that the further the distance travelled, the offending rate decreases exponentially (Rengert et al, 1999). Proponents argue that the further away from home an offender is the more factors intertwine to prevent crime. For example, if the offender does not have access to transport, their ability to commit offences further away is diminished. Or, as some neighbourhoods tend to have a certain community or ethnic base to their population, this can mean that the offender would stand out, again reducing the likelihood of them wishing to commit an offence in that area.

REFLECTIVE PRACTICE 2.5

LEVEL 4

Think about a time you have travelled elsewhere previously unknown to you, whether that be on holiday, a time you moved home, or even at a family member's house.

- What behaviours do you think you displayed to others that show you were unfamiliar with the area?

- Did this impact on you as you tried to go about your everyday behaviour? (Even if it was just trying to find where the toilet was.)

- Now consider you were a burglar in the area and wanted to commit a couple of offences while you were there. Would any of the behaviours or difficulties make it harder to offend and why?

Over time, however, the concept of distance decay has been adapted and more recently as the idea of a 'buffer zone' was introduced. This states that although the distance decay applies, it only does so after a 'buffer zone', which is typically around their home or anchor point. The argument for this is that, for ease of living, people do not want to annoy their neighbours and chances of being caught are higher as they are more recognisable in the immediate vicinity of their own homes.

There are of course some issues with this theory. For example, it presumes an offender has one single home or anchor point, which as we have seen from the start of this chapter, offenders can have a range of different issues, and this may not be the case at all. Additionally, it presumes that an offence has a key defined location but does not take into account online crime or even offences that are transient such as joyriding or even offences that take place on trains (O'Leary, 2011).

When it comes to investigating offences, we also must consider how this might be applied in the real world. We can see that the distances vary wildly depending on transportation and other factors, including those independent to the offender. As such, when it comes to catching criminals without having mapped out the mobility of each area and hoping the offender fits into the characteristics of an 'average offender', it cannot be reverse engineered to assist policing: in effect, it becomes little more than an interesting model.

LOCATING OFFENDERS

Criminological theory does not just tell us why an offender commits criminal acts, it can also help provide some ideas on being able to locate offenders. While the distance decay model might be able to give us an idea of an offender's anchor points, one growing area of research is in geographic profiling.

One concept is that of marauders and commuters, which was first proposed in Canter and Gregory's (1994) work. Marauders can be described as people whose home we can identify by drawing a circle using the two offences most geographically spread committed by the same offender. Commuters are those who offend in a decentralised manner; this is less common, and their offending behaviour takes place around a common route for them whether that be their commute or bus route (Canter and Youngs, 2008). For an investigator using this, the key therefore is to identify what kind of offender you are dealing with so you can narrow down your search and confirm whether all the offences have been committed by the same offender. From experience, I would suggest this is not done purely by MO as it is quite easy to link offences this way forgetting that offenders share techniques, especially if they have been in prison together, and it is far better to have a firm evidential link to confirm it is the same offender. In addition, profiling should only be done by those trained and, depending on the offence type and seriousness, profilers are available to law enforcement in England and Wales. While there is no harm in you producing a hypothesis on a basic level, I do not suggest your efforts to track down suspects solely rest on profiling.

Regarding other methods to track down suspects, I am sure throughout your career you will learn to fine-tune the art. However, for the more troublesome people here are a few suggestions. Please remember I cannot put anything sensitive here but there are endless opportunities. My top tip would be to ask a friendly DC.

- Mobile phones – in our current world, people are permanently attached to their phones whether they are smart or not. If you can link an offender to a phone, it opens a world of opportunities for you.

- Money – everyone needs money to exist, even those that shoplift for a living. Banking enquiries can assist in seeing where people frequent to do their shopping and how they get their benefits.

- Social media – this can help in several ways. Firstly, it is important to remember that people often have more than one social media account and their names are not as they are on their birth certificate. Once you have identified an account or two, you can do the obvious enquiries regarding logon details, but you can also look at their friend lists. If we can start to frustrate friends with our enquiries to find them sometimes suspects magically present themselves.

SUMMARY OF KEY CONCEPTS

This chapter has looked at a wide range of topics regarding suspects.

- The age of offending curve shows a spike of offending at a young age, which tails off as the offenders get older.

- The concept of the revolving door shows how previous offending can be used as an indicator of future offending.

- Many offenders experience common traumas or negative issues in their lives.

- There are a range of criminological theories that can be considered to help you understand offenders and offending.

- Lombroso argued for biological reasons and likened criminals to degenerates and even compared criminals to monkeys.

- Broken windows theory argues that people commit crime when they do not feel people care about what is happening.

- Labelling theory states that when you call someone or an act they commit bad, this in some ways becomes self-fulfilling.

- Rational choice theory argues that offenders weigh up the pros and cons of offending in their head before deciding whether to commit an offence and choose to do so if it is in their best interests.

- Routine activity theory creates a triangle of crime with an offender able to commit an offence, a suitable target for the offence and lack of guardians for the target. By addressing one or more parts of this triangle, we could prevent crime taking place.

- The Chicago School of Criminology introduced a zonal model with five areas, which highlighted that different offences took place in different areas and that friction between different areas also encouraged offending.

- The distance decay theory argues that offenders typically offend more when closer to their anchor point/home. However, the concept of the buffer zone means there is, in effect, an area they would not touch.

- Offenders may be located using geographic profiling and the commuter and marauder model in addition to other methods.

- Policing practice requires you to understand and use the above information to your advantage. No single theory will encompass all offending or offenders but being able to draw from a toolbox of theories can make your policing practice more effective.

CHECK YOUR KNOWLEDGE

1. Explain what ACEs are.

2. Which theory uses a 'crime triangle' and what are the three factors?

3. Explain what the distance decay theory argues.

4. What is broken windows theory?

5. Describe how you could locate an offender.

Sample answers are provided at the end of this book.

FURTHER READING

Carrabine, E, Cox, P, Lee, M, Plummer, K and South, N (2009) *Criminology: A Sociological Introduction.* Abingdon: Routledge.
I can only talk about my experiences with the second edition but when it came to the criminology part of my undergraduate degree this book was a huge reason I passed. It breaks theory down into easy-to-digest language and more importantly it provides a good level of detail to allow you to reference it at an undergraduate level.

Cullen, T and Wilcox, P (eds) (2013) *The Oxford Handbook of Criminological Theory.* Oxford: Oxford University Press.
This is a fantastic book to read if you want to read in more detail about criminological theory. This book is a collection of works that break down the theories by type and go into great detail. A heplful read should you need to write any essays.

Newburn, T (2017) *Criminology.* Cullompton: Willan Publishing.
This is a good stock book to have if you want to learn about criminology and it covers most areas in an understandable manner. I do, however, provide a word of warning: it is everyone's go-to book so, when it comes to your assignments, markers can look on it negatively as it does not show a depth of reading.

CHAPTER 3
PROCEDURAL JUSTICE

LEARNING OBJECTIVES

AFTER READING THIS CHAPTER YOU WILL BE ABLE TO:

- know what procedural justice is and why it is important to policing;

- show how you can apply procedural justice in your work and the impact it has;

- understand what happens if the relationship between police and the public goes wrong.

WHAT IS PROCEDURAL JUSTICE?

Procedural justice is not something that is overly complex or particularly revolutionary, but it is fundamental to carrying out your policing duties fairly. Understanding what procedural justice is and how to apply it to your role will hopefully result in the public being more understanding and engaged with whatever policing process you are doing at the time.

Gau (2013, pp 188-9) described the need for procedural justice by stating that: *'Any agency which possesses coercive authority over another segment of society must devise a rationale which explains to those people why it's right to submit to that authority.'* In short, this means that the police, who exert authority over segments of society, must find a way to explain to those people why they should allow the police to do their job. If we look deeper, this links back to the second and third Peelian policing principles:

- the ability of the police to perform their duties is dependent upon public approval;

- police must secure the willing co-operation of the public in the voluntary observance of the law in order to gain and maintain respect (Gov.uk, 2012).

Academics have broken the concept of procedural justice down into four key components. For procedural justice to exist there must be:

1. dialogue that encourages citizen participation in proceedings prior to an authority reaching a decision;

2. perception of neutrality in decision making;

3. dignity and respect throughout the interaction;

4. conveying of trustworthy motives.

(Mazerolle et al, 2015, p 246)

ENCOURAGING CITIZEN PARTICIPATION IN PROCEEDINGS

Encouraging citizen participation in proceedings essentially means giving the participant a voice. You do not necessarily need to do what they say, but it is important that they are involved in what is taking place and allowed to express their views. In practical terms, this could involve putting them in your position and explaining the options you have, asking them what you should do and then explaining the option you have gone for and why. At its core, this is about people not feeling like they are being forced but rather that they have a say.

NEUTRALITY IN DECISION MAKING

This relates to the public feeling like there is no hidden motivation for or against them, which might impact on the outcome. If you ever watched the *Tom and Jerry* cartoons you can imagine Tom's frustration when the homeowner returned and always took Jerry's side as he was the innocent mouse victim, when actually many of their interactions were tit for tat. By listening to both sides and then taking action we come to hopefully not only a better decision but also one where people do not feel victimised.

DIGNITY AND RESPECT

Treating people with dignity and respect should be everyday practice for you as a police officer in line with the Code of Ethics, in particular acting with authority, respect and courtesy (College of Policing, 2014). This element, I personally believe, has the greatest impact on how the interaction will go, especially if we consider 'Betari's box' (Figure 3.1).

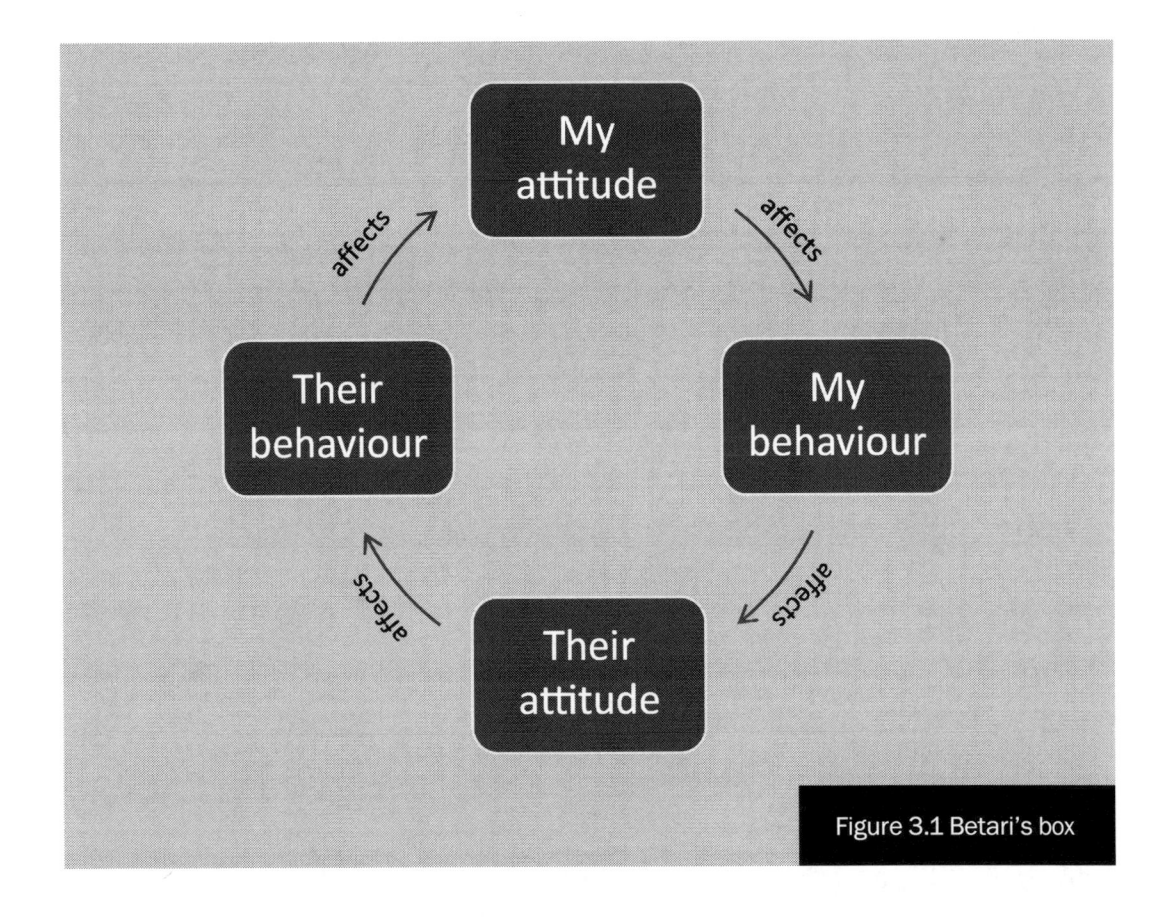

Figure 3.1 Betari's box

As you can see from Figure 3.1, by altering your thought processes and behaviour you will impact on the individual you are interacting with and their behaviours. Therefore, by treating people with dignity and respect we prevent a spiralling negative situation from occurring, which would in turn affect our conduct.

CONVEYING TRUSTWORTHY MOTIVES

Conveying trustworthy motives is about showing the public that you are not acting with unworthy reasons and that what you are doing is ethically the right thing. Although this should be the case anyway, obviously demonstrating this to the member of the public is what makes the key impact here. In essence, this comes down to your communication skills.

POLICING SPOTLIGHT

Imagine you were stopped for going through a red light, despite you being absolutely certain it was green (maybe amber) and the officer did not listen to your perception of what happened and they just gave you a ticket and said they did so because they were short on tickets this month and did not want to get in trouble. How would that make you feel?

Then imagine if, however, you had an opportunity to apologise and explain your actions and the officer explained the safety implications. They explained their rationale for giving a ticket over words of advice and that you could have been taken to court. They highlighted it is becoming a regular issue at this set of lights and a seven-year-old boy was run over last week, because someone was not looking, and everyone being stopped is being treated the same. Despite the outcome being the same, would you be more willing to accept the ticket and move on?

CRITICAL THINKING ACTIVITY 3.1

LEVEL 5

Consider the national decision-making model, which is frequently used by the police.

- How does the concept of procedural justice interact with the use of the model?

- Does knowing about procedural justice change the outcome of your decisions? What does it change?

REFLECTIVE PRACTICE 3.1

LEVEL 4

Think back to a time in your life when you made a decision that impacted on others and that they could have felt was unfair (for example, being picked last on a sports team).

- On reflection, did you make the decision unfairly or was the way the process was conducted add to the feeling of others being victimised?

- Using that reflection, is there any way that could have made the process feel fairer, even if the outcome were the same?

WHY DOES PROCEDURAL JUSTICE MATTER TO POLICING?

Procedural justice is not about making the easy decision or avoiding conflict, but about ensuring that the perception of the decision making is fair and ethical and the public do not feel excluded from it. In the hope that your decision making is already ethical and fair, the key difference is spending time getting 'buy in' from the person involved. The College of Policing (2013) state that:

> without the cooperation of the public, policing in developed democracies would become essentially unworkable ... by improving public perceptions and increasing trust through fair decision making and positive public interaction, the police service can enhance its legitimacy.

As a consequence, therefore, we need and have used procedural justice to ensure that the public remain onside with the police and we are seen as legitimate going forward.

Policing, however, is not just about having to avoid riots. Once you start to serve as a police officer you may reflect on comments you receive because of victim satisfaction or other feedback mechanisms. Research in policing consistently indicates that evaluations of police legitimacy are based on people's views on the way police treat them and is independent of how well the police do their job. As a result, good application of procedural justice could improve their opinions of the police and you.

When it comes to dealing with difficult members of the public, and I can guarantee in your service you will come across a few, people's views about legitimacy can influence their willingness to accept decisions, can leave people feeling happier with the decisions and authority and can shape compliance behaviour (Hinds and Murphy, 2007). As a result, procedural justice is not just about keeping members of the public happy but also making your role easier by taking the time to nurture good relationships with both victims and perpetrators of crime.

Procedural justice does not just impact on a person-to-person level but can operate more broadly. Baird (2001) refers to public services as having to have a 'running tally', which increases with pleasing or understandable decisions, and which develops into a reservoir of good will that can be called upon should something disagreeable happen.

EVIDENCE-BASED POLICING

Reisig and Lloyd (2009) conducted a study in Jamacia that tested the hypothesis that adolescents who view the police with a higher sense of procedural justice are more willing to assist the police with their enquiries. The study surveyed 289 students across Jamacia and examined a number of factors in regard to procedural justice. The research supported the hypothesis. In addition, a higher sense of procedural justice was also linked to a greater sense of police legitimacy. What was interesting, however, was that despite the two factors being linked, police legitimacy on its own was not enough to provide a statistically significant link to police engagement, albeit the article does state that further research on this might be required.

What this study does not explain, however, is how officers created this sense of procedural justice and this is because it has to be applied on a case-by-case basis. It is also a difficult thing to empirically measure or create control groups for, especially in a policing context. But what this research does show is that putting the effort into interactions creates a more willing sample of people.

ARE THERE ANY ISSUES TO PROCEDURAL JUSTICE BEING USED?

When applied properly and effectively, procedural justice can only help with policing and its legitimacy. When it comes to its implementation into your practice, you must do so with a sense of realism as it is important to remember that research in policing cannot be relied upon to avoid all issues. For example, it will not stop people being angry or even disagreeing with the decision made. What it may do, however, is diminish the protests you come across.

While the four elements are helpful in creating buy in, there is little written by the authors as to how to go about this or putting these principles into practice. Policing by its very nature can be difficult and interactions can take place in pressured situations for both you and the member of the public so, while these are good principles, their application in context could be difficult. The College of Policing (2021b) have gone some way to providing advice through their communication guide, which itself refers to procedural justice, but its application at times when you are under pressure, you are tired from being on nights and you have not had a toilet break since you have started is another matter.

Finally, while the principles illustrate that there needs to be an element of fairness to proceedings, people's perception of fairness is personal and variable and can fluctuate from situation to situation. Different people also view different procedural elements as key to defining procedural justice (Tyler, 2004, p 448). If this is the case, how are you as an officer to know what is important when trying to enact this in your practice?

POLICING SPOTLIGHT

Imagine you have been called to your local high street. The person you have stopped matches the description of a person reportedly having a knife in their pocket. As a result, you are going to subject them to a stop and search under S.1 Police Criminal Act 1984. At the end of this search, imagine that you find nothing and you believe it was a false report. As a member of the public, how would you feel having been searched?

REFLECTIVE PRACTICE 3.2

LEVEL 5

- Write out a script for the two versions of this stop:
    1. the first for a search that fulfils the legal criteria required of you and not much else, for example, abiding by GO WISELY;
    2. the second where you are super nice, abide by GO WISELY and explain every step of the process, making an effort to build rapport with the individual and using empathy to explain the reasons for the stop.

- Looking back on those two interactions, if you were a member of the public, how would you feel after each interaction?

- Despite the physical process, legality and outcome being the same, explain why there could be different perceptions of the fairness of what took place.

CRITICAL THINKING ACTIVITY 3.2

LEVEL 6

Think about another common interaction you might have with the public (such as an arrest).

- Is there anything in policy, law or Authorised Professional Practice (APP) that you feel helps to improve the feeling of procedural justice?

- Do you think that these steps are enough? Is there anything else you could do to help improve perceptions of the process?

- Is there anything written that you think goes against procedural justice? If so, why does it? Is there any way it can be framed to help alter perspectives?

The above exercises demonstrate that your everyday policing practice directly impacts on people's perceptions of procedural justice and the police organisation as a whole. Remember your first interaction with someone could be their only interaction with the police on which they may base their entire opinion of policing.

POLICING SPOTLIGHT

WHAT HAPPENS WHEN IT GOES WRONG?

One example where a large section of society felt policing went against them with little sense of procedural justice was in the build-up to the Brixton riots, which took place between 10 and 12 April 1981. A review following the riots was published in the Scarman report (Lord Scarman, 1981), which conducted a deep dive into the circumstances leading up to the riots, including the socio-economic circumstances and the policing tactics used. This report is said to be the birth of the Police and Criminal Evidence Act 1984 (PACE), which governs so many policing activities today.

According to the Scarman report, the disorder started when officers were trying to catch up with a youth whom they had seen had serious injuries and they feared would die if not attended to. When officers eventually caught up and attended to him, a crowd formed and criticism started when they decided to not let him move prior to an ambulance attending as they believed that doing so would only make the injury worse. This increase in tension led to additional police resources being sent to the scene to help manage the crowd. The report itself says:

> *Young Black people ... lacked confidence in the police. The worst construction was frequently put upon police action, even when it was lawful, appropriate and sensible.*
> (Lord Scarman, 1981, p 45)

The next day there was an increased police presence in Brixton. As part of the patrols, one set of officers conducted a stop search, due to the officer noticing something odd in a driver's socks when they were speaking to them. Initially, it was a person search and the person being searched was compliant, but a crowd formed. The vehicle was then searched and the driver protested due to fears that an item would be planted, which resulted in the crowd asking the officers to leave the driver alone. When an officer arrested another person for obstructing their duty, it became violent with a crowd of over 150 actively resisting against officers (Lord Scarman, 1981, pp 45–51). This led to public disorder spanning a number of days.

It is worth noting that the report also cites an operation 'Swamp 81' as an element that added to the frustration among the local community. This operation took place just before the riots, with 10 squads of five to 11 officers patrolling the area to tackle the high levels of street crime, and led to over 900 stops and over 100 arrests. The public and local community leaders were not informed of this operation in advance and these interactions led to high levels of tension in the area, which seemingly was ignited as a result of the above two interactions (Lord Scarman, 1981, pp 94–6).

While a single use of procedural justice in this matter may not have prevented the disorder, the report clearly states that the residents of the local population lacked trust and confidence in policing. Routine use of procedural justice would have assisted in easing or even prevented the longer-term tensions, and in regard to the stop search, better engagement from the driver may have prevented his demonstrations and the crowd turning against the police.

SUMMARY OF KEY CONCEPTS

This chapter has discussed the following key concepts.

- Procedural justice should become everyday practice in the way you approach policing decisions. It centres around the following four key principles.

    1. Conversation with those involved to get their engagement with decision making before a decision is made.
    2. The perception that the decision made is a neutral one.
    3. You show dignity and respect to the individual involved.
    4. Demonstrating that the interaction has trustworthy motives.

- By using these principles, we ensure that the public remain engaged with the process and are more willing to accept decisions made.

- This makes the initial interaction easier and helps police satisfaction. Consider that we rely on the public to be accepting of us and our power and without consent policing would not be able to function.

- When procedural justice is not used, however, we can see from the Brixton riots that law and order could begin to break down. At that time, there was a huge disconnect between the public and the police, which led to distrust and a small interaction resulted in widescale damage and disruption.

- When using procedural justice, it is important to remember that it is not a magic bullet to resolve conflict.

- Research has also shown that differing groups see different elements of the interaction as important to ensuring their perception of organisational justice making it even more difficult for officers to focus on getting what is important right.

- It does highlight the importance of acting within the Code of Ethics as set out by the College of Policing.

CHECK YOUR KNOWLEDGE

1. In a sentence describe what procedural justice is.

2. What are the four main principles of procedural justice?

3. Why is procedural justice important to your policing practice?

4. What are the key issues when trying to implement it into your practice?

Sample answers are provided at the end of this book.

FURTHER READING

HM Inspectorate of Probation (2020) The Evidence Base – Models and Principles – Procedural Justice. 18 December 2020. [online] Available at: www.justiceinspectorates.gov.uk/hmiprobation/research/the-evidence-base-probation/models-and-principles/procedural-justice/.
The Justice Inspectorates have created a simple to understand guide about procedural justice, which you might find helpful if you need clarification. In addition, they have produced a handy video to explain the benefits of procedural justice and the key principles, which is also available on that link. Despite this being done with a probation and custodial lens, its content is still applicable to policing and shows procedural justice can be used throughout the CJS.

College of Policing (2021) Communication. 18 November 2021. [online] Available at: www.college.police.uk/guidance/vulnerability-related-risks/communication.
When it comes to your policing practice, the College of Policing Communication guide gives a helpful steer as to good practice and what pitfalls to avoid. By following this guidance, you should naturally bring elements of procedural practice to life, without having to over complicate it.

Tyler, T R (2004) Procedural Justice. In Sarat, A (ed) *The Blackwell Companion to Law and Society* (pp 435–52). Oxford: Blackwell Publishing.
This is a more academic read into procedural justice. However, it explains the elements in great detail and would be useful if you need to write or wish to learn more about procedural justice.

CHAPTER 4
POLICING, SOCIAL CONTROL AND THE ROLE OF OTHER AGENCIES

LEARNING OBJECTIVES

AFTER READING THIS CHAPTER YOU WILL BE ABLE TO:

- understand what is social control;

- explain how policing is not just the role of the police;

- understand the role of other agencies in the policing landscape and the CJS and their practical links;

- explain how these groups contribute towards social control.

INTRODUCTION

Policing does not work in isolation; you will be aware that it plays a key role within the CJS. However, have you considered that the police are not the only people to police? Security guards and traffic wardens, to name a few, also play a policing role. It is important for the police to understand how they fit into this landscape of agencies as well as the wider CJS.

This chapter explores what social control is and who is involved in policing and introduces you to the CJS. Having done so, it then looks at how various elements of the CJS exert a level of social control.

WHAT IS SOCIAL CONTROL?

Social control is described as '*means by which conformity to social norms might be achieved*' (Gooch and Williams, 2007, p 338). You will notice that crime or deviance is not mentioned in this definition and that is because the idea of social control is much broader than just criminality and can, as an example, include areas such as health. Social control steps away from other sociological ideas regarding behaviour, which are based around a more individualistic pursuit, and focuses more on the broader backdrop of individuals' actions. Social control's key idea is that society regulates itself towards a set of agreed goals. As such, social control is seen as the opposite to coercive control, which is the idea that social organisation rests on predominately the use of force or threat of force (Janowitz, 1975).

Rather than the use of force, social control manifests itself in two main forms. The first, informal, is typically seen when neighbourhoods work within themselves to regulate behaviours. This can be seen when parents tell their children off to maintain social boundaries or neighbours keeping an eye on each other's addresses. This informal control ensures the status quo of accepted normality continues without the need for more serious action.

This predictably contrasts to the second form of social control, which is formal. This is seen when set processes are undertaken to maintain the control, such as when we see prosecutions and a case go through the CJS (Drakulich and Crutchfield, 2013). Formal social control is the focus of this chapter.

REFLECTIVE PRACTICE 4.1

LEVEL 4

- Consider the idea of social control in society. What examples of society trying to ensure achievement towards certain goals can you see in regard to:
    - health?
    - environmental issues?
    - crime?
- In the examples you have noticed are these informal or formal acts of social control?

Sample answers are provided at the end of this book.

THE ROLE OF POLICING

Policing is part of social control and can be carried out in many different settings. Reiner (2000) stated that policing *'occurs universally in all social situations in which there is at least the potential for conflict, deviance or disorder'* (Davies et al, 2005, pp 141–2).

The police function is unique, but the concept of policing is not just isolated to this singular body and the idea of policing being separated out among various organisations is known as *'pluralised policing'* (Crawford, 2008, pp 147–8). An example of pluralised policing can be seen in areas of London where a company, My Local Bobby, formed in 2016 when policing resourcing budgets were stretched. This company provides a neighbourhood policing style service by offering commercial security options to residents and even has a sister company that specialises in conducting private prosecutions (My Local Bobby, 2022). Ironically, one article argued that the rise of these kinds of services and agents employed by those away from the state was originally one of the main arguments for the introduction of the Police Community Support Officer (PCSO) (Kempa and Johnston, 2005) who now have become commonplace within neighbourhood teams, albeit much reduced of late due to financial constraints placed upon forces.

More recently, the community safety accreditation scheme (CSAS), and the railway equivalent (RSAS), takes a further step towards police embracing pluralised policing agencies. The scheme allows companies to be accredited by a local police force who then subsequently accredit individuals. These people must be vetted and approved by the chief police officer in the area they work, but in exchange for them doing so, allows them access to additional low-level powers in law (Police Crime Prevention Initiatives, 2022).

POLICING SPOTLIGHT

PC Snow, a neighbourhood officer, is aware of frustration within the local community following a range of parking issues in and around a new shopping centre in town. The shopping centre, despite being new, seemingly does not have enough parking and that overspill is having wide effects on the community.

Despite PC Snow being aware of these issues, he has other priorities to attend to including incidents of violence and investigations, which carry far higher risk despite numerous low-level public order offences now being reported.

As a result of this, PC Snow speaks to colleagues at the local council who arrange for some parking wardens to attend the area and proactively enforce parking infringements. In addition, PC Snow also speaks to the shopping centre to encourage their security staff to become part of CSAS in the hope that they can start to assist in dealing with the low-level public order matters reported.

CRITICAL THINKING ACTIVITY 4.1

LEVEL 5

Imagine you were in the position of PC Snow.

- What are the benefits of engaging with other bodies who can assist with policing?

- What are the potential challenges?

- How might you overcome some of these challenges?

- Do you think it is in the interests of the police to encourage others to have powers?

Despite this pluralisation of policing, the role of a police constable still plays a unique role in policing with the College of Policing (2023) stating that: *'constables play a critical front-line role in the prevention and detection of crime and the criminal justice system'*. The latter part of the quote highlights the key difference the police service has compared with others who are part of the pluralised model of policing in that many others do not have that interaction with the wider CJS. This interaction will be discussed in the next section.

THE CRIMINAL JUSTICE SYSTEM

The CJS is complex and although private prosecutions do take place most criminal cases follow a similar process. Figure 4.1 illustrates how just one investigation can engage with multiple agencies within the CJS.

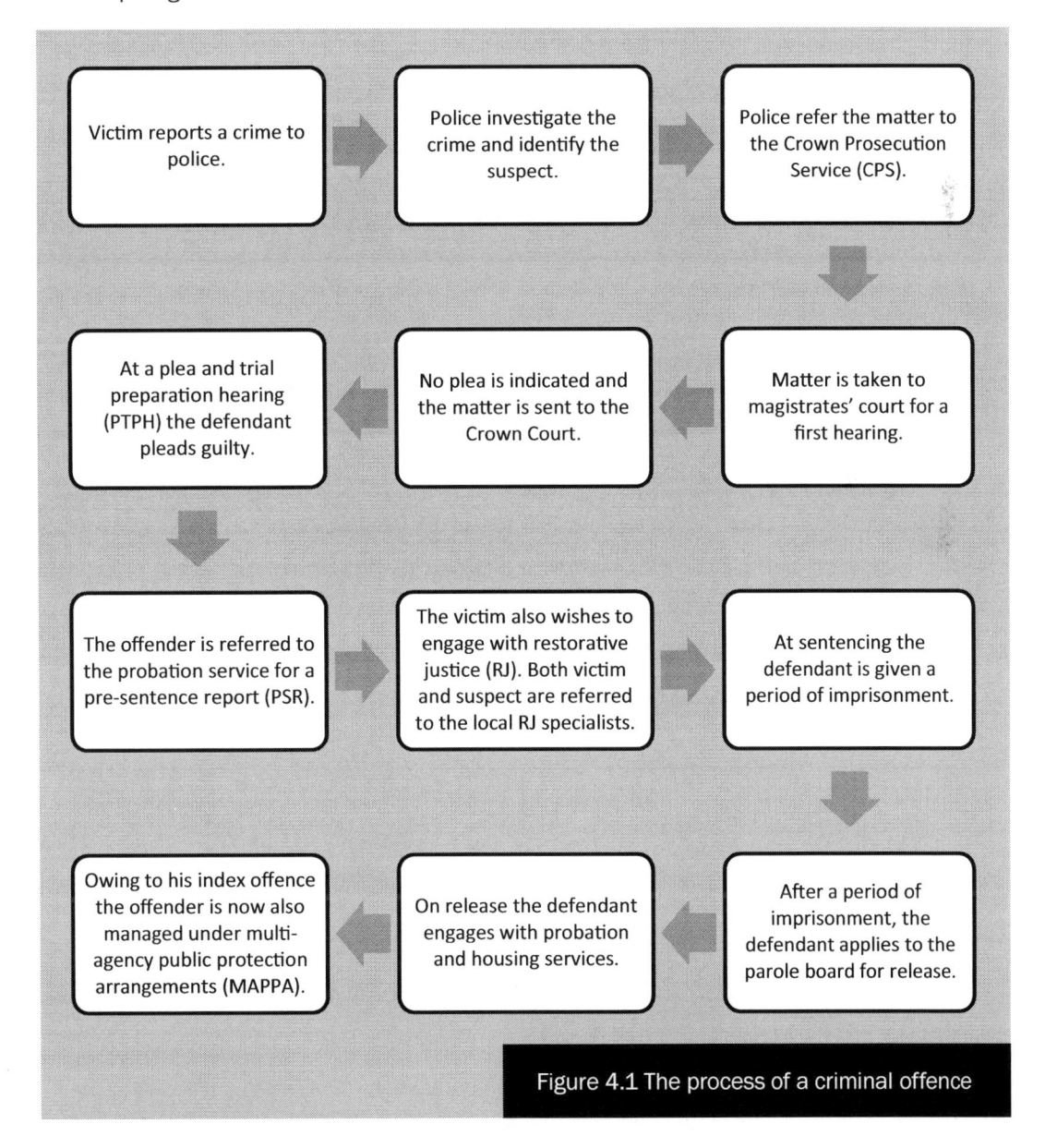

```
Victim reports a crime to police. → Police investigate the crime and identify the suspect. → Police refer the matter to the Crown Prosecution Service (CPS).
↓
At a plea and trial preparation hearing (PTPH) the defendant pleads guilty. ← No plea is indicated and the matter is sent to the Crown Court. ← Matter is taken to magistrates' court for a first hearing.
↓
The offender is referred to the probation service for a pre-sentence report (PSR). → The victim also wishes to engage with restorative justice (RJ). Both victim and suspect are referred to the local RJ specialists. → At sentencing the defendant is given a period of imprisonment.
↓
Owing to his index offence the offender is now also managed under multi-agency public protection arrangements (MAPPA). ← On release the defendant engages with probation and housing services. ← After a period of imprisonment, the defendant applies to the parole board for release.
```

Figure 4.1 The process of a criminal offence

As you can see, there is a plethora of different agencies involved in a relatively straightforward criminal case. Each agency is discussed further so you can understand their roles fully and understand how the police interact with these agencies. Having discussed this, their interaction with the concept of social control is also explored.

THE POLICE

Given that this is a police-based book, a fair amount could be written about the police service's role in the CJS. To many, policing is seen as the gateway to the CJS and for most criminal matters the police are involved with the investigation. Police officers are afforded a reasonable amount of discretion when dealing with matters and decide in most cases whether to send a casefile to the CPS for onward progression. This idea does raise some interesting conversations about who administers justice. However, without the police to effectively filter what matters continue through the process, there would be no management of risk or proportionality. In statute, there are many different offences. Not all of them need to be put before a court and the police's role in part is to manage that volume.

Policing does not just engage in criminal convictions. Policing also engages in ways to reduce crime through crime prevention, and works with other agencies to divert would-be offenders and potential victims to reduce their risk, such as through social services referrals. A common crime reducing example is seen through schemes such as Neighbourhood Watch, which, as part of its activities, seeks to influence informal control behaviours. Policing is also involved in out of court disposals, all of which seek to strike a balance between dealing with criminality and being proportionate as to what enters the court system and preventing crime.

When it comes to social control you will notice therefore that while the police are involved in the formal method they also influence and engage with many informal methods.

THE CROWN PROSECUTION SERVICE

The CPS is the prosecution agent for criminal trials that have been investigated by the police and other agencies. They are independent of the police and decide which cases should be prosecuted and what charges should be brought, prepare cases for court and help support victims and witnesses through the court process (CPS, 2022).

When working in policing, it is important to have a good working relationship with the CPS. When taking matters to court, they are the ones who make decisions and as such working closely with them ultimately provides better results.

Within policing, often one area of frustration is regarding decision making in cases by the CPS. Police investigators, understandably and rightly, invest a lot of time and effort and often have pride in the cases they present to the CPS and, on occasion, the decision returned is not the one anticipated. In some regards, this is a good thing. It shows the independence of the CPS, who should coldly look at evidence and decide based on what is presented, both protecting court time and avoiding falsely inflating victims' hopes, as well as being an effective countermeasure to any potential police biases.

It is important when presenting cases to know how the CPS come to a decision. As an investigator, this means you can present the information in a way that is most beneficial for all those who review it and, where relevant, highlight important pieces of information.

The Code for Crown Prosecutors (CPS, 2018), while a lengthy document, highlights the two tests used when making prosecution decisions. Details are also included in *Police Procedure and Evidence in the Criminal Justice System* (Archer et al, 2023), but for ease are summarised here. For the majority of cases, the full code test is utilised (Figure 4.2). This test can be used when all reasonable lines of enquiry have been completed or, if prior to an investigation being completed, when the prosecutor is satisfied that any further material obtained is unlikely to affect the application of the test. This test is made up of two key elements: the evidential stage, which asks whether there is enough admissible evidence to provide a realistic prospect of conviction; and the second is the public interest, which tests whether prosecution is required in the public interest. Only if both tests are passed is a prosecution case raised.

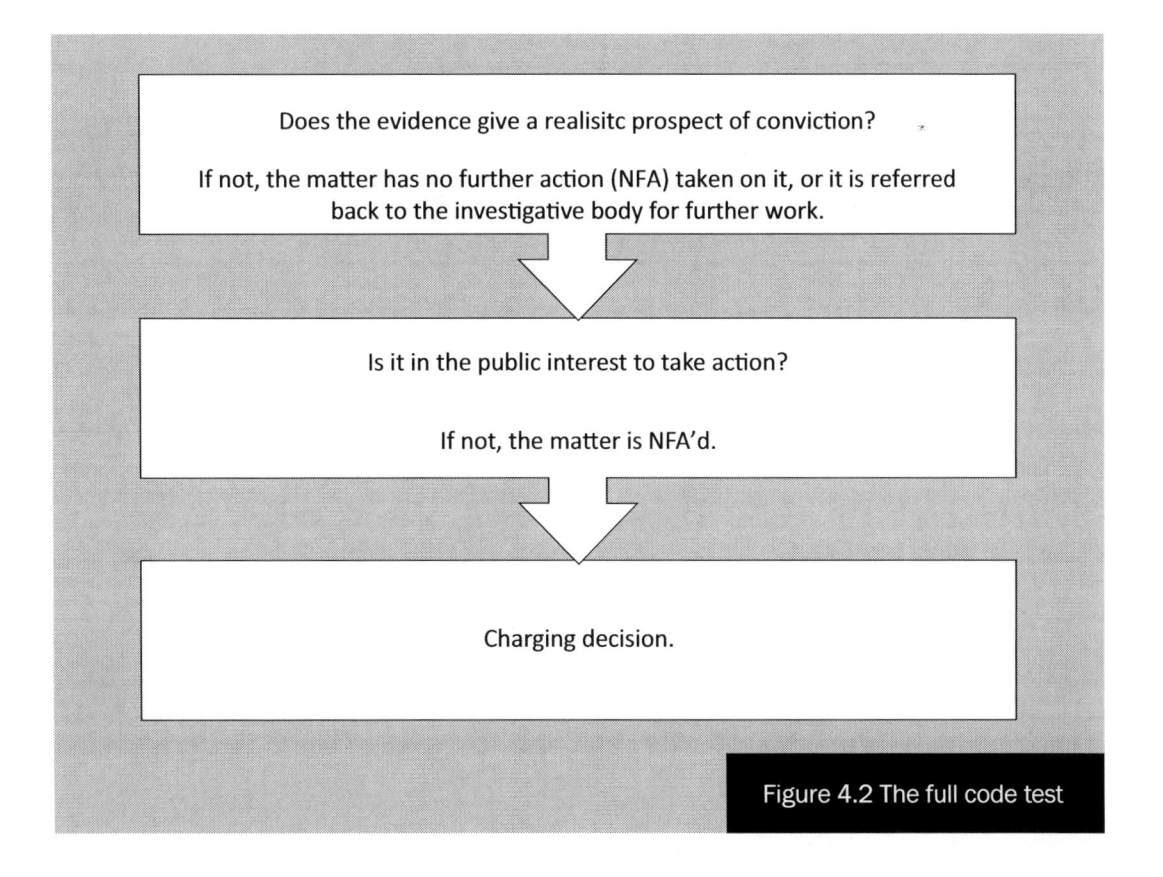

Does the evidence give a realisitc prospect of conviction?

If not, the matter has no further action (NFA) taken on it, or it is referred back to the investigative body for further work.

Is it in the public interest to take action?

If not, the matter is NFA'd.

Charging decision.

Figure 4.2 The full code test

The second test that can be used is in cases where the full code test has not been met but the seriousness of the matter means that an immediate decision should be made. Given the nature of this test, it is far more complex as without the full casefile several variables are still at play for the prosecution. This, understandably, makes it riskier for the CPS to decide and could potentially mean the wrong person could be imprisoned for an offence. As a result of this increased risk, to utilise this test there are five conditions that need to be met:

1. reasonable grounds to suspect the person to be charged has committed the offence;

2. further evidence can be obtained to provide a realistic prospect of conviction;

3. the seriousness or the circumstance of the case justifies the immediate charging decision;

4. there are continuing substantial grounds to object to bail, and it is proper to do so;

5. it is in the public interest to charge the suspect.

When working on these cases, where time is of the essence, it is important for the police to be able to have these tests in the back of their mind. This will help you prioritise relevant lines of enquiry, aid decision making and reach whatever the desired outcome is.

CRITICAL THINKING ACTIVITY 4.2

LEVEL 5

Consider the evidential tests for prosecution.

- Do you think this is a form of social control?

- Do you think it is right that the CPS decide what is and what is not in the public interest?

- What factors do you think the CPS should consider when making this decision?

- As an investigator, how might you highlight these factors to them?

THE COURTS

His Majesty's Courts and Tribunal Service (HMTCS) operate the courts in England and Wales for both the civil and criminal sides. This book focuses on the criminal side.

Courts operate in a hierarchy (Figure 4.3). This means that the decisions of higher-up courts influence those below and the higher up the decision has come from, the more influential it is over other matters. This concept is known as judicial precedent (Elliott and Quinn, 2007). All cases start at the bottom-most court but, depending on the seriousness of the matter, it may just be for a fleeting moment as the lower-level courts cannot deal with all offences.

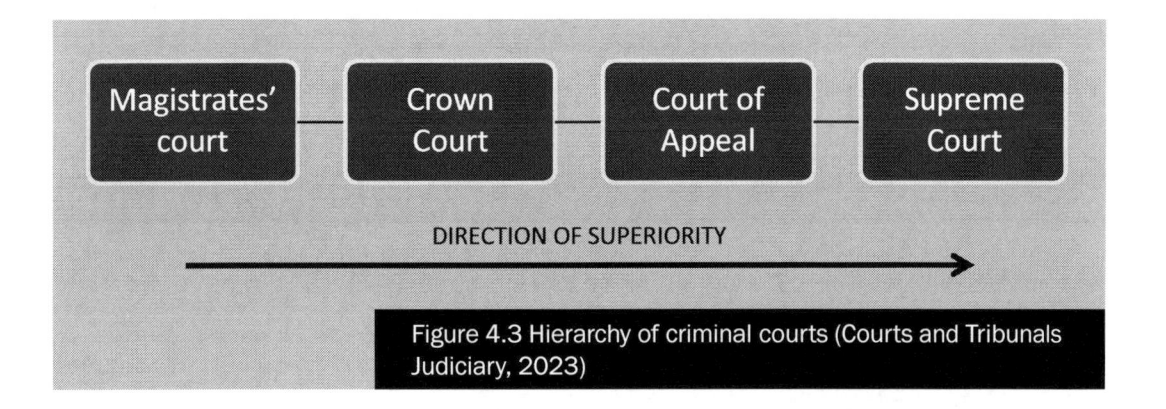

Magistrates' court — Crown Court — Court of Appeal — Supreme Court

DIRECTION OF SUPERIORITY →

Figure 4.3 Hierarchy of criminal courts (Courts and Tribunals Judiciary, 2023)

You can see a more in-detail diagram of the UK Courts System in Chapter 7 of *Police Procedure and Evidence in the Criminal Justice System* (Archer et al, 2023), also in this series. Because of this hierarchy, most matters are dealt with in the Magistrates' court and have no need to go elsewhere. Serious matters known as indicatable-only offences are generally dealt with in the Crown Court. The Court of Appeal hears appeals regarding:

- convictions in the Crown Court;

- sentences given by the Crown Court;

- confiscation orders imposed by the Crown Court (HMCTS, nd).

The Supreme Court is the final Court of Appeal in the United Kingdom for criminal matters but also hears other important civil matters that are of the highest importance (Supreme Court, 2022).

As an investigator, you will very rarely see the latter two courts in your career. Although, if you start to deal with more serious and complex matters, then the chances will increase as generally with complexity comes sentences, which the defendant may challenge specifically on points of law.

PROBATION

The probation service work closely alongside the court and are responsible for sentence management in England and Wales in the form of accredited programmes, unpaid work and the structured interventions handed down as part of sentences (Probation Service, nd). In the scenario depicted in Figure 4.1, you see that they also carry out pre-sentence reports (PSRs). These are reports produced for the courts prior to sentencing to ensure they are furnished with the facts relating to the offender required to make an informed decision. When it comes to the monitoring of sentencing, the probation service also inform the court should conditions of a sentence have been breached and they feel it is proportionate to pursue the breach. When considering formal social control, you can see how probation weighs heavily on convicted individuals' conformance and the consequences of them not doing so.

PRISON SERVICE

HM Prison Service operate the majority of the prison estate within England and Wales. At the time of writing, the most recent prison population was 81,806 prisoners. In just a three-month period, 15,817 first receptions entered into the prison system and just 11,650 people were released (HM Prison and Probation Service, 2023).

Prison is not just a place simply to 'lock people up'; it can also be used for education, which is increasingly important when you consider that typical educational attainment of those incarcerated is below that of the general population. As an example, it is reported that 48 per cent of prisoners have a reading age at or below an 11-year-old. This increases to 65 per cent for numeracy and 82 per cent for writing skills. More alarmingly from a rehabilitative view is that half of all prisoners do not have the skills required for 96 per cent of jobs and only one in five can complete an application form (Canton et al, 2011).

An example of the education work provided can be seen in a project that utilised the arts to help engage prisoners with literacy and numeracy learning. Across three different types of prisons – youth offenders, long term and general population – one study analysed a range of different programmes. The study found that prisoner engagement with the arts reported increased confidence and awareness of what the prisoners were good at and motivated them to engage in learning literacy, numeracy and communication skills (Tett et al, 2012).

Education is not the only intervention that can be conducted in prisons. Those detained are also increasingly likely to have poor mental and physical health compared with those in the general population (Baybutt et al, 2009). As a result, a range of studies have been conducted to help improve this situation. One study reviewed yoga and found that those that engaged had lower self-rated psychological distress. Another study reviewed the effectiveness of CBT, which also improved psychological well-being. When it came to drug misuse, again, successes were seen especially in those schemes whereby care continued in the community (Fazel et al, 2016).

While this chapter is not an in-depth review of the effectiveness of prisons, what is clear is that prison can offer a diverse range of options to engage with those sentenced with the hope to better their futures but also encourage elements of social control beyond that of criminality, whether that be educational attainment, rehabilitation or better health and well-being.

CRITICAL THINKING ACTIVITY 4.3

LEVEL 5

Consider the range of interventions potentially offered within a prison.

- Given that the person is there for a criminal matter, do you think there is value in offering these?

- How do these programmes interact with the concept of social control?

PAROLE BOARD

The parole board is an independent body that reviews prisoners and risk assesses them to determine whether they can be safely released into the community prior to the completion of their full sentence (Parole Board, nd). The parole board is made up of a range of people including judges, probation officers and psychiatrists (Davies et al, 2005). Utilising the information available, they review each case on application.

One research study identified that, on the whole, parole boards over-estimate the risk of reconviction, in particular sex offenders (Hood et al, 2002). Nevertheless, their key aim is to make sure they only release prisoners who are deemed to be safe and of little risk to the community.

OFFENDER MANAGEMENT

Offender management is complex and the main body involved in its administration is the probation service. When it comes to probation, there are two approaches. The first is rehabilitative, which sees probation as an alternative to punishment, and the second is punitive, which sees it as an alternative form of punishment (Weiss, 2001). The probation service have already been discussed above; however, they often work closely with policing when it comes to multi-agency public protection arrangements, also known as MAPPA.

MAPPA

MAPPA is not a body in itself but a mechanism in which agencies work together. The main responsible authorities for this agreement are the police, prison and probation services. In addition to these, other bodies have a duty to co-operate and these are generally agencies that impact on an offender's life, such as housing, education and social care (HM Prison and Probation Service, 2022).

There are three categories of offender under MAPPA.

1. Category 1 – Registered sex offenders who have been convicted or cautioned since 1997 for certain offences.

2. Category 2 – Violent and other sexual offenders who received a custodial sentence of 12 months or more since April 2001 or hospital order or are the subject of disqualification from working with children.

3. Category 3 – Other offenders considered by the responsible authority to pose a risk of serious harm to the public (Wood and Kemshall, 2007).

The different categories dictate the level of involvement the MAPPA teams have and enable others within the CJS to know at a glance what kind of offenders they are. The key to this joint agency working is to address the reasons why people offend, help keep them on track and take action when this does not happen.

POLICING SPOTLIGHT

The management of offenders is important as in some cases they pose a significant risk to the public. One such example of this was the case of Thomas Smith, who was subject to offender management having been previously found guilty of a sexual offence against a 10 year-old girl in England. Despite this engagement, he raped and murdered another 10 year-old girl and her mother who were his neighbours in Scotland (BBC News, 2010).

In the review of the MAPPA process following the murders, it was observed that he had deceived a number of people, including the police, while they were trying to manage him. The review stated that despite being deemed as high risk, the rationale for his enhanced risk was not clear. If the true details of his original crime were fully considered, despite already being high risk, a more thorough risk assessment would have been carried out, which may have meant a different approach to him. The report also highlighted deficiencies in the social services report about him and the police failed to stick to their plan of doing more unannounced visits than was required, which may have afforded them more opportunities to get involved with him as an offender (East Ayrshire Chief Officers Group, 2011). As a result of this review, several recommendations were put in place to prevent cases such as these happening again.

YOUTH OFFENDING TEAMS

Youth offending teams (YOTs) supervise 10–18 year-olds who either have been sentenced by a court or have been dealt with out of court by the police. Much like the MAPPA arrangement, it is a partnership between the police, local authority social care and education, probation service and health services. They are utilised in several ways, including the provision of RJ, reparation of harm following a crime and seeking to mitigate the risks of further re-offending (HM Inspectorate of Probation, 2017). You may notice many similarities with MAPPA; however, the approach is somewhat different. They aim to treat the offender as a child first and as such take a more holistic approach to addressing their issues.

An example of this approach is illustrated in a study into YOTs, despite their initial interaction with a young person being due to their involvement in criminal acts. To help prevent re-offending, health workers were utilised within the team. In certain cases, they ensured the young people had access to a GP, dental and mental health services as required, which in the article was described as '*therapeutic surveillance*' (Brooker et al, 2022). What it did mean was that the young person's basic needs were being met and that a range of agencies had intervention points for various matters to ensure that potentially small issues were unlikely to escalate and cause offending.

EVIDENCE-BASED POLICING

An example of this holistic approach can be seen in the HITZ programme. This is run by individual rugby clubs but under the umbrella of Premiership Rugby.

HITZ aims to use sport to improve the personal lives and employability of disadvantaged young people aged 14–24. It can provide a traineeship, education opportunities and employability skills and provides mentorship around that (London Irish, nd).

It is aimed at people with poor exam results, physical and mental health issues, unsettled homelives, alcohol or drug misuse issues or those that have been in trouble with the police, by providing an alternative approach to traditional education routes. Results have shown approximately 84 per cent of participants have improved their functional mathematics and English, and over 80 per cent have progressed in further education, employment and training (Premiership Rugby, nd).

The above scheme is just one of many sporting groups that provide schemes to select groups of young people and highlights the value of engagement with young people to help towards their long-term contribution to society and ultimately attempting to ensure they remain within social boundaries.

CRITICAL THINKING ACTIVITY 4.4

LEVEL 4

Think about the HITZ programme.

- How does this fit in with social control?

- Why do you think professional sportspeople involve themselves in these matters?

- Do you think there is benefit to non-government bodies becoming involved with these young people?

THE CJS AND SOCIAL CONTROL

When reading this chapter, you may have originally considered that the CJS contributes towards social control in the traditional way, namely that it deals with breaches of the law and deals with the offender accordingly. However, you can see that it contributes to it in many more ways.

Policing, while being a gateway to the CJS, also deals with a range of non-criminal matters and ensures that information is shared with other agencies such as social services so they can, for example, ensure children are being looked after correctly.

The CPS also provide counterbalance, ensuring that even if an offence has taken place this does not always mean that it will be prosecuted. The public interest test is an interesting mechanism in this and provides a court-like power to the prosecuting agent.

You have seen that a young person who engages with a YOT is not just dealt with as a criminal but, on occasion, is checked to ensure their health needs are met and steps are taken if that is not the case. Similarly, within MAPPA housing advice and support services are involved to ensure that those released are not left homeless and therefore seen to act outside the social norms.

It is quite easy to think that social control is all about crime and those stepping outside those boundaries. However, as you have discovered, the CJS contributes more to social control than merely being a formal act of control.

SUMMARY OF KEY CONCEPTS

This chapter has discussed social control and the criminal justice system.

- Social control is more than just crime; it is about ensuring people adhere to social norms.

- Social control comes in two forms: formal and informal.

- Policing is not just down to the police but happens within everyday society.

- The CJS has a number of players involved within it and at times a range of them work together to ensure social control.

- Even within the prison system, steps are taken to ensure a form of compliance with social control. The parole board in particular ensure those that are released have taken steps and have a decreased risk of re-offending.

CHECK YOUR KNOWLEDGE

1. What is the hierarchy of courts?

2. List at least three agencies involved within MAPPA.

3. Describe the two tests the CPS use to decide whether to prosecute an individual.

4. What is social control?

Sample answers are provided at the end of this book.

FURTHER READING

College of Policing (2023) Professional Profile: Police Constable. 31 January 2023. [online] Available at: https://profdev.college.police.uk/professional-profile/police-constable/.
The role profile for a police constable shows the breadth of skills and tasks an officer has to undertake. An awareness of this is key to truly understanding what being a constable is all about. The current police recruitment system refers to the competency and values framework (CVF). As a result, each role profile links into the CVF and explains what areas you need to evidence to potentially get a job. As a consequence, should you ever apply for a police role, you would strongly benefit from knowing and understanding the CVF and the role profile.

CPS (2018) The Code for Crown Prosecutors. 26 October 2018. [online] Available at: www.cps.gov.uk/publication/code-crown-prosecutors.
Police officers can get frustrated with decisions made by the CPS. However, to give the CPS the best chance of agreeing with the charging decision suggested it is extremely helpful to know the code of practice they use. By doing so, you are able to present your cases in a way that addresses what they are looking for and, when you do so, if you were to disagree you will have a far more likely chance of being able to appeal.

Elliott, C and Quinn, F (2007) *English Legal System*. Essex: Pearson.
This title, while maybe not a criminological text, most certainly has a more recent edition than the one I have used. This book is an essential guide to understanding the England and Wales legal system. A core text in some A level law programmes, it is accessible and comprehensive should you want a deeper look into law.

CHAPTER 5
POLICING AND POLITICS: ACCOUNTABILITY, POLICE POWERS AND THEIR REGULATION

LEARNING OBJECTIVES

AFTER READING THIS CHAPTER YOU WILL BE ABLE TO:

- discuss how policing is held to account;

- describe the creation of police powers;

- explain how these laws are shaped by other agencies such as the HMICFRS and the College of Policing.

INTRODUCTION

Police in England and Wales police by consent. This comes from the Peelian principle, which states that the power of the police to fulfil their functions and duties is dependent on the public approval of their existence (Gov.uk, 2012). In order to maintain this approval, there are a number of mechanisms in place to ensure the police remain on the right side of public approval.

This chapter shows how these different mechanisms interact with the police and ensure that policing, if required, evolves to meet the ongoing public need. Having done so, it then explains how a new law is made for you to have an insight into the process.

POLITICS

Policing and politics have an interesting inter-connected relationship. Operational policing is supposed to be free of political influence; however, you will soon see how the two connect and one influences the other. It is worth noting that there have been entire books dedicated to this relationship. This chapter cannot provide that level of detail but what it can do is highlight the key discussion points for you to research further should you want to in the future.

Savage (2007), in his book on police reform, highlights that for police reform to take place the political climate needs to be one that is receptive to the messages coming through. This is not just whether the politicians are listening but whether it is politically suitable to reform the police in that relevant area at the time. You can see an example of this is with the recent Conservative government who argued that, in essence, the police cannot be trusted. Consequently, a wealth of reforms were put in place in an effort to try and reinstate the loss of confidence (Schaap, 2018).

Conversely, if you look at the previous Labour government's approach, they were elected on the auspices of being 'tough on crime, tough on the causes of crime'. Their reforms were much more looking at 'what works' in crime reduction and utilising both traditional and new agencies to tackle community-related issues as well as the introduction of new roles such as the PCSO to tackle lower-level issues (Hope, 2005).

From these two examples alone, you can see the contrasting approaches, both of which brought about reform but did so in specific areas that suited the government at the time. Given the closeness in time between both governments you could argue that the messages regarding diminishing confidence in policing were being received by the Labour government but not acted upon as it eroded their message of reducing crime.

MEDIA INFLUENCE

Politicians are not the only ones to set the political agenda. Owing to the nature of politics, they must be seen to react to what the public want and a key way they see these concerns and messages is through the media. It is worth noting, however, that the media can also use this influence to suit their own goals. In one piece of research, a HMIC (now known as the HMICFRS) inspector highlighted that following arrests of certain members of the media in regard to phone hacking, the media had turned against the police (Schaap, 2018). Consequentially, it makes sense if you are seeking to make change not to rely on the media entirely and use a range of sources.

POLICING SPOTLIGHT

SARAH EVERARD

A recent example of the media and the public's influence on policing to ensure they reform accordingly can be seen after the Sarah Everard murder.

Sarah Everard was murdered by Wayne Couzens, a stranger to her and a serving police officer. He initially stopped her under the auspices of being an undercover officer, an act that was witnessed by people who thought he was going about his formal police business and in doing so he used his handcuffs to inhibit her ability to escape. He then drove her to Kent where he proceeded to rape and murder her before dumping her body, having attempted to burn her body inside a fridge (BBC News, 2021).

The outcry following his abhorrent acts was understandable as was the media coverage. What followed was a wealth of reforms: an example of which is the increased scrutiny and work towards tackling Violence Against Women and Girls (VAWG), which in the national framework for its delivery specifically mentioned Sarah Everard (College of Policing and NPCC, 2021).

It was not just police investigations that were reviewed. Couzens, being a serving officer, along with another case involving a serving officer, highlighted the need for increased police vetting, which has subsequently been introduced (Nickolls, 2022).

While this is just one example, if you look back on policing history where large reforms have taken place you can see landmark cases bringing about change. Elsewhere in this book, the Brixton riots are discussed, which is another example. However, in all of these cases you can see a wealth of media interest and subsequently further interest in similar matters that potentially would have been missed.

The police do exert some control over the media, despite the argument that sometimes the media is against policing. Owing to the nature of policing, often the media relies on the police to provide them with information about incidents. This means that the police can effectively starve the media of information if it suits their objectives. Chermak (1995) argued that police often use the media and frame stories in a way that strengthens their position as a crime fighting institution. This is because the public crave crime news and the interaction requires limited resources. This raises an interesting question as to the value of the media when it comes to holding the police accountable. If the police arguably frame stories in a way that is beneficial to them and the media relies on their information, how exactly can the media truly hold them to account?

REFLECTIVE PRACTICE 5.1

LEVEL 5

Have a look at a recent media story involving the police or a crime. As you do so consider the following.

- How much of the information comes from the police?

- Does this article positively portray policing?

- If not, where does the information around the police come from?

- Do the answers to the questions change if you look at different types of story, whether that be a sentencing, appeal for information or another police-based article?

POLICE AND CRIME COMMISSIONERS

Police and crime commissioners (PCC) are a relatively new element to the police accountability framework in England and Wales and replaced the former police authority model. PCCs are elected individuals who can be associated with political parties and are tasked with holding local chief constables and their forces to account. Prior to their implementation, the Conservative Party manifesto argued that police authorities were invisible and unaccountable, and the role of an elected individual will give people democratic control over the policing priorities (Conservative Party, 2010).

The PCC's remit includes:

- appointing and dismissing a chief constable;

- setting police and crime objectives in an area;

- setting the force budget;

- bringing together partners to ensure joined up local partnerships;

- contributing to national and international policing capabilities set out by the home secretary

(Association of Police and Crime Commissioners, nd)

CRITICAL THINKING ACTIVITY 5.1

LEVEL 6

- Consider what impact having political party influence might have on the role of the PCC.

- Do you think that this political party influence will change if the same party has a majority in parliament?

The introduction of PCCs, however, is not without criticism. While the idea of an elected individual is heralded as a step towards democracy, in some cases police oversight has gone from 17 individuals to just one, raising the question as to whether the oversight is effective or representative of the area the police serve (Mawby and Smith, 2013). In a different study, a chief constable argues that there was better oversight in the previous model as '*you had a balanced group of people representing different areas, different parties*' (Shannon, 2020, p 917).

Another area of growing criticism is the public's engagement with the PCC and election process. On average in the 2021 election only 33.2 per cent of the electorate turned out to vote (Danechi and Tunnicliffe, 2021). Which, if compared with the general election in 2019, where the turnout was 67.3 per cent (McInnes, 2020), highlights a stark difference. This lack of engagement could be seen as devaluing the democratic gains argued when PCCs were introduced. Conversely, despite the lower turnout, this level of democratic involvement is far more than was ever seen during the police authority era.

REFLECTIVE PRACTICE 5.2
LEVEL 6

Consider the previous PCC election or, if you could not vote, think about your answers if an election were to take place soon.

- Do you remember/know what each candidate stood for?

- How much did you hear about the election before the actual day?

- Did you vote in line with your usual voting habits?

- What do your responses say about the effectiveness of electing PCCs?

THE HMICFRS

The HMICFRS were formally known as the HMIC, as until recently they did not have supervision of the fire service. They are an independent inspectorate, which looks at the efficiency and effectiveness of police forces across England, Wales and Northern Ireland. They also, on occasion, will inspect British Overseas Territories and Crown Dependencies on request from their governments (HMICFRS, 2022).

As part of their role, the HMICFRS conduct regular Police Effectiveness, Efficiency and Legitimacy (PEEL) assessments, which give one of five grades to each police force, much like an Ofsted (Office for Standards in Education, Children's Services and Skills) inspection for schools. They grade a range of areas from providing a service to victims of crime, recording data about crime to tackling workforce corruption (HMICFRS, nd). These reports are accessible on the internet and are often reported on in the media and as such hold the police to account by ensuring the national standards are abided by and that other forces are compared against one another. Given the media reporting, this can often put pressure on the PCC and local chief constable to act to make improvements where appropriate.

Another part of their inspection programme is thematic inspections; these usually look across a number of forces and are often commissioned following increased scrutiny or political interest in an area of policing where improvements could be made. These reports look to improve policing overall and as such do not just suggest recommendations for policing practice but also areas where the Home Office or others might want to invest or improve. An example of this is in a recent review into youth violence where recommendation 2 was that the Home Office *'should further develop existing joint evaluation and learning for violence reduction units to share learning with each other'* (HMICFRS, 2023, p 12).

The impact of HMICFRS inspections can at times be limited. Loveday (2017) noted in his article that regarding online crime in particular, the HMIC highlighted the issues for future demand in the area but despite this, forces did not adequately respond.

Despite this criticism, the HMICFRS can be seen to hold forces to account. Its regular inspections provide a reference point for forces to target improvements and their thematic improvements seek to improve policing practice. Their research is often reported upon and, as a result, while allowing policing to improve itself, it also utilises the mechanisms already discussed within politics and the media.

THE COLLEGE OF POLICING

The College of Policing have a broad role within policing but when it comes to police accountability, they provide a number of unique functions. First of all, they set standards for police practice such as through the APP, other standards and the Code of Ethics. They also have a role in supporting professional development through a number of programmes and finally they seek to share knowledge and good practice through products like their crime reduction toolkit and research map (College of Policing, nda).

These standards do not hold policing directly accountable. However, it is important to remember that the standards being in place means that police forces are inspected against them. For products such as the APP, while not being law, if practice departed from the guidelines and something went wrong, questions would be asked. These standards are created utilising evidence-based approaches and are not therefore 'pie in the sky' concepts.

Police accountability would struggle without standards to assess against. Inspection would become a competition between forces rather than a tool to help drive changes utilising the latest available evidence. As such, it is important to know the College of Policing's role in police practice.

POLICING SPOTLIGHT

STOP AND SEARCH

Consider the highly discussed topic of stop and search. This area is often the subject of essays.

When it comes to accountability, there are a range of different facets to the police use of stop and search. On a day-to-day basis, the use of the power is written into law and its application is subject to scrutiny both in the courts and if someone feels aggrieved by the application of the police power through the police complaint system, and sometimes both.

In addition to the legislative framework, the use of stop and search is accompanied with codes of practice, as are other PACE powers, such as police detention. These are not law, in the same way that the power given to police is in statute. However, they are highly persuasive and any departure from these codes can be used in court as an illustration of oppressive practice and, as a consequence, can lead to exclusion of evidence.

Alongside this is the College of Policing APP. This is similar sounding to the codes of practice but in practice is more of a guide on the good use of stop and search. It details when police use of the power is most likely to be fair and effective including descriptions on the legal application of the power and guidance on transparency (College of Policing, 2022a). When it comes to complaints, often actions are reviewed against the APP and the codes of practice, both of which are publicly accessible meaning everyone could know what the police should be doing in an interaction.

The HMICFRS regularly review the use of stop and search due to its controversial nature. In a recent review into the use of the power, while they noticed that training had improved substantially, it transpired that reviews of body-worn video took place far too rarely meaning people were not able to review their own practice or have feedback given to them (HMICFRS, 2021a). This scrutiny ensures that forces challenge themselves for constant improvement.

On occasion, however, we see instances where a number of these agencies combine to approach a complaint. In May 2021, the Criminal Justice Alliance raised a super-complaint regarding the use of 'suspicion-less' stop and search powers (Ali and Champion, 2021). This complaint was reviewed by the Independent Office for Police Conduct (IOPC), the HMICFRS and the College of Policing to ensure an adequate response was provided.

CRITICAL THINKING ACTIVITY 5.2

LEVEL 5

Consider the amount of scrutiny stop and search has had.

- Do you think this is justified?

- Why do you think so many organisations are interested in its use?

- Do you think, given its success, it is appropriate to keep using the power?

POLICE COMPLAINTS

This chapter does not intend to explain the intricate nature of the police complaints process. However, if you do wish to read more about the processes involved, Hutton et al (2022) is a good starting point.

Police complaints are the most direct way that individuals who feel aggrieved by the powers of the police can address them and hold officers to account. While police complaints in some regards are similar to those in other public sectors, the unique powers officers have, including the ability to restrict an individual's liberty, quite rightly require additional levels of scrutiny (Seneviratne, 2004).

Most police complaints are dealt with locally by the police force's professional standards department. However, the IOPC investigate serious matters and, on occasion, direct investigations utilising local police resources.

Effective management of police complaints is important as it ensures the police remain accountable and provides trust in the process. Lord Scarman, in his review, heard that many dissatisfied citizens did not complain because of a lack of confidence in the process due to the then heavy police influence in the process (McLaughlin and Johansen, 2002). If you think back to the policing by consent model, the public must have confidence in the police complaints process for the consent of the public to remain.

EVIDENCE-BASED POLICING

Being accountable to the public through police complaints is not the only way to improve accountability. Improvements in technology utilised by the police have also provided opportunities to improve accountability through other means.

Ariel et al (2017) examined the use of police body-worn video cameras and the effect on citizens' complaints against the police across the world. Following the introduction of the cameras, the study noticed a significant drop in complaints against officers from an average of 1.2 complaints per officer per year to 0.08 – an approximate drop of 93 per cent.

This is a drastic change and could indicate several things. It could mean that the officer is aware that they are being recorded by either their own camera or a colleague's and consequently temper their behaviour accordingly preventing the requirement for the complaint. Alternatively, the person bringing the complaint would also know they are being recorded and as such the bringing of a vexatious complaint is pointless as the video evidence will clear the officer in question.

In one randomised study in the USA, the use of body-worn videos was compared with a number of factors including use of force and officer discretion and it found no statistically significant variance whether the camera was used or not. In fact, it slightly indicated, but not in a statistically significant way meaning no firm conclusions can be drawn, an increased use of force when officers have cameras. The suggestion being that officers are used to being regularly recorded by members of the public and therefore their behaviour did not need to change (Yokum et al, 2019). However, as with most studies when it comes to police use of force, the data relied upon is self-reported and as such may not represent a true and accurate picture.

You can see from the body-worn video technology that police complaints, and the technological advances, have allowed for greater oversight on police powers, which ensures officers remain accountable. A lot of officers often view getting police complaints as a matter of course, during their policing career. In your own career, however, while they might cause frustration and anxiety due to the processes involved, remember they are also an opportunity to reflect. You cannot and will not please everyone in policing; however, the complaint process is there to make you accountable and learn. Utilise the opportunity to look back and consider things you might change in your practice going forward.

POLICING SPOTLIGHT

PC Borne was in their tutoring period when unfortunately, they were assaulted in an arrest and received minor injuries.

The prisoner was dealt with in custody and charged with assault on an emergency worker. However, immediately upon their release, the suspect submitted a complaint regarding the use of force against them.

PC Borne, alongside their tutor, reviewed the body-worn video footage, in line with their force policy. On review, they did notice that their force processes were not 100 per cent adhered to and there was some learning to be taken from it as it was PC Borne's first occasion where they used force during an arrest.

REFLECTIVE PRACTICE 5.3

LEVEL 5

Imagine that you are in the position of PC Borne.

- How would you feel having been assaulted and then receiving a complaint?

- How would you approach responding to a complaint when you know there were some improvements to be made?

- Do you think that this would have an impact at court?

CITIZEN OVERSIGHT

Alongside the above methods to maintain police accountability there are also a number of other established methods that involve members of the public. The below are not exhaustive albeit they are the more common forms. Some forces, as an example, also offer ride-along schemes to assist members of the public gain insight to the role. While this does not necessarily directly hold officers accountable, they do provide a range of benefits. As well as giving insight, it also allows the police to have casual interactions with sections of the community they might otherwise not engage with in their role. This helps increase understanding of sections of the community and answer often challenging questions that are at the forefront of the public's mind.

INDEPENDENT ADVISORY GROUPS

Independent advisory groups (IAGs) are voluntary groups made up of members of the public who are independent of the police. They contain a mix of people, some of which may have a specialist interest in a particular area of policing or may be general members of the public keen to provide feedback to the police. These groups will often review how the police handle major investigations as well as incidents and issues that impact local communities (Hampshire and Isle of Wight Constabulary, nd). It is argued that the principal function of an IAG is to safeguard against disadvantaging any section of the community through lack of understanding, ignorance or mistaken belief and it does so with a community focus (Aplin, 2023).

These groups are described as being critical friends to policing and hold a unique role. While they get privileged information about policing, their role is to provide evaluation, to question and to challenge established methods of practice. However, in the research presented by Dixon (2020, p 694), one participant in an IAG was quoted saying:

> *In the main the people that come along are police-lovers, which is very nice but it makes it difficult for us to be critical friends. They are not critical, they are friends.*

In your career you may get an opportunity to run an IAG. It is important to ensure that the voices heard are the ones that provide most value to the IAG. This may not be the convenient voices available to the police but for true accountability the challenging viewpoint needs to be heard.

LAY CUSTODY VISITORS

Another form of civilian involvement in ensuring policing accountability is seen in the role of lay custody visitors. Their role evolved from a recommendation in the Scarman report and a key aim is to prevent harm, provide public reassurance custody is safe and ensure human rights obligations are being met (Independent Custody Visiting Association, nd). This model ensures that custody environments have regular visits, which maintains good standards for detainees and ensures that there is a level of public scrutiny in what is typically and understandably a closed environment.

There are criticisms of the model utilised. In Kendall's (2022) study, it was noted that although timings of visits were 'random' often they were, in fact, highly predictable as they required the availability of volunteers. In addition, when the volunteers did attend, they were never observed asking about the decision to take legal advice or for those who required an appropriate adult whether an appropriate adult had been spoken to, which is a key legal protection afforded to detained persons. Much like the criticism raised against the IAGs, it was also highlighted that custody visitors exhibited closeness towards those they were supposed to ensure were doing their job, this in turn undermines their critical function.

These are just two examples of civilian oversight in policing. Despite their flaws, they do still provide policing access to speedy and localised feedback, which they may not have otherwise received, especially in cases where serious lessons need to be learnt.

What is clear is that police have a myriad of different tools in order to keep themselves accountable and ensure the law and powers that they exercise are done so appropriately and in the spirit in which they were intended.

THE CREATION OF LAW

Often because of holding the police accountable or following debates on policing, new legislation is introduced to either tighten existing powers or tackle a new and emerging problem. It is important to understand how law is created. You might during your career come across situations that you or a member of the public think should be addressed by a new law but yet it is not. Often, this process is seen to be slow, which can be frustrating, but some knowledge in what takes place might assist you when explaining to a member of the public.

While there are a number of variances in the creation of law, many start in a similar way through the introduction of a bill to either the House of Commons or the House of Lords. Any member of parliament can create a bill; however, their position in government might dictate the route it takes and how much time it gets allocated. Understandably, the more time it is allocated the more chance it has of being successfully debated and passed into law.

In parliament, the process shown in Table 5.1 typically takes place for primary legislation.

Table 5.1 Creation of law process

First reading	This is a formal stage in which the title of the bill is read out and there is no debate.
Second reading	This contains a debate on the main principles of the bill and a government minister will explain the reasons for its creation.
Committee stage	This is a much more in-depth line-by-line review and allows written and oral submissions. This stage may introduce amendments based on the discussions.
Report stage	In this stage only amendments are discussed.
Third reading	This takes place in both houses generally on the same day. This discusses the amendments.
Further readings	These may be required if edits are required to ensure agreement between the two houses on the text of the bill.
Royal assent	This is now very much a formality in the law-making process; however, it must be completed before the law can be enacted.

Cabinet Office (2013); UK Parliament (nd)

As you can see from the above, although certain laws can be created quicker, the creation of primary legislation must go through many processes, which can take some time. Consider also how many bills are likely to be brought before parliament and you can understand why change is often slow.

POLICING SPOTLIGHT

UPSKIRTING

A recent example of the need to change legislation can be seen with the emergence of upskirting. This is the trend that often in public locations an offender would point a camera to see up a skirt to see what the person was wearing. The issue with the law at the time was that it was created at a time where legislature was trying to tackle the 'peeping tom' scenario and therefore voyeurism only dealt with people who spied on people in private and for sexual gratification (McGlynn and Rackley, 2017).

This change in behaviour is argued to be a classic example of how technology outpaced law reform and, despite law makers seeking change in June 2018, it took until February 2019 for the act to receive royal assent (Ministry of Justice, 2019a) and until April 2019 to become an offence that could be charged and sentenced with up to two years' imprisonment (Ministry of Justice, 2019b).

This method of predatory behaviour had been subject to some media interest for some time with an article on the issues of convicting these individuals in America being published in 2014 (Grossman and Friedman, 2014). Yet, it took five years for it to be addressed in UK law.

REFLECTIVE PRACTICE 5.4

LEVEL 5

Imagine you were a victim of upskirting in 2014 prior to it becoming an offence. You have reported the matter to the police but despite them identifying an offender, no further action could be taken.

- How would you feel?

- As an officer what could you say to a victim who was in this situation?

- How would you advise the victim to try and encourage them to make change?

SUMMARY OF KEY CONCEPTS

This chapter has discussed an array of areas regarding policing and politics.

- The police are held to account through a range of mediums. The public, politicians and other bodies all play their part.

- The PCC holds considerable power in the governance of policing.

- The College of Policing, while not directly scrutinising policing, plays an important part in ensuring police practice is kept up to date and evidence based.

- Civilian oversight in policing, while not new, does play an important part in keeping the police accountable to the public but also ensures the police are aware of issues facing their communities.

- The creation of law is a long process, which takes a number of steps. Through the upskirting example, we have seen how long it can take from becoming an issue to being directly addressed in law.

CHECK YOUR KNOWLEDGE

1. What is the role of the PCC?

2. How does the political sentiment towards policing impact on the policy decisions made?

3. How do body-worn cameras ensure that the police remain accountable?

4. How do the HMICFRS ensure the police remain accountable?

Sample answers are provided at the end of this book.

FURTHER READING

Bowling, B, Reiner, R and Sheptycki, J E (2019) *The Politics of the Police*. Oxford: Oxford University Press.
This book covers a range of topics covered in this chapter in a lot more depth and is a good and well-reviewed resource for any academic study. The book looks at policing transnationally, which can broaden your academic outlook on policing.

HMICFRS (nd) PEEL Assessments 2021/22. [online] Available at: www.justiceinspectorates.gov.uk/hmicfrs/peel-assessments/peel-assessments-2021-22/.
The PEEL assessments are a good way to gain a quick and in-depth insight into your local force. You can see insights into emerging issues and reforms put in place to address them. Interestingly, you can also review previous assessments, which help show the trajectory a force is heading in.

Mawby, R I and Smith, K (2013) Accounting for the Police: The New Police and Crime Commissioners in England and Wales. *The Police Journal*, 86(2): 143–57.
This article provides an interesting review into the role of PCCs. Given their relatively new status, there is not a lot of research about them and this presents the issues well.

CHAPTER 6
PRINCIPLES OF CRIME PREVENTION

LEARNING OBJECTIVES

AFTER READING THIS CHAPTER YOU WILL BE ABLE TO:

- explain the principles of crime prevention;

- utilise them to provide advice to the public;

- understand 'what works';

- explain how criminology interlinks with these theories.

INTRODUCTION

Crime prevention is important: Sir Robert Peel put prevention of crime first in his policing principles. Therefore, it is important for you to know and understand what works, how it works and when is best to utilise different crime prevention methods. Policing is busy so if you can prevent a single crime, you are not only safeguarding a victim but also lessening the burden for you and your colleagues in the future.

Crime prevention has a number of principles. This chapter explores all 10 of them before discussing two common approaches to crime prevention: situational crime prevention and crime prevention through environmental design (CPTED).

PRINCIPLES OF CRIME PREVENTION

There are 10 principles of crime prevention:

1. *target hardening;*
2. *target removal;*
3. *reducing the means;*
4. *reducing the payoff;*
5. *access control;*
6. *surveillance;*
7. *environmental change;*
8. *rule setting;*
9. *increasing the chances of being caught;*
10. *deflecting offenders.*

(West Yorkshire Police, nd)

Many of these principles seem straightforward; however, their creative implementation to differing crime challenges is where the artistry of crime prevention really shows. Throughout this chapter, a range of examples are displayed that often required someone to look at the problem creatively to produce the solution. You may also see that while examples are used to highlight one principle, they may in fact use a range of them, highlighting the strength of the intervention, with more than one opportunity to be effective.

TARGET HARDENING

The first principle is target hardening, which aims to make it harder for potential targets to become victims of crime.

POLICING SPOTLIGHT

A classic example of this is seen in a Home Office practice report (2004), which looked at the crime prevention challenges of the student population. Statistics showed that households containing people of student age were at an increased risk of being a victim of burglary. The report reviewed several approaches and noticed that students were less afraid of crime and as such were not taking simple measures such as locking their doors. Therefore, to target harden successful projects used that information in their implementation, such as utilising self-closing locks. Another example of student target hardening was in a project in Sheffield. Terraced houses in the student housing market often had a shared alleyway, which allowed unseen access to around four addresses at a time. To help remedy this, alley gates were installed at addresses to mitigate the risk of burglary.

One concern of target hardening is that of displacement. This is the idea that crime will simply move to another location or target once you put preventative measures in place. A study in Australia examined this following the introduction of target hardening measures at banks in Victoria. They were concerned that the steps taken might mean that offenders move to other venues such as convenience stores or other states. However, following a review, this was not seen to be the case although the study did not compare banks that had different levels of security (Clarke et al, 1991).

REFLECTIVE PRACTICE 6.1

LEVEL 5

Think of a residential address you have attended recently, whether that be through work or even a family member (grandparents' addresses are generally good for this task), and select two types of crime, such as burglary and internet-enabled crime.

- What target hardening for these offences could you see or know are in action?

- As an officer attending these addresses, what solutions could you suggest to further enhance the target hardening?

- If you provided crime prevention advice, how did you approach it?

- What is the best way to give that advice if someone is already a victim of crime?

TARGET REMOVAL

Target removal works on the simple premise that you cannot commit an offence if the target no longer exists. While, in principle, this sounds easy, its practical application is not that straightforward. For example, you cannot simply suggest to university students to get rid of their laptops because they keep getting stolen. You can, however, suggest that laptops are kept in a special secure room while they are away on holidays to minimise theft thus removing them from the target locations (Home Office, 2004). A common MO for burglary is to take car keys that are kept close to the front door of homes, meaning that after entry escape can be swift. An example of target removal in this case is to move the keys elsewhere in the house or ensure they cannot be seen close to the door.

EVIDENCE-BASED POLICING

An example of target removal was in the NHS (National Health Service). They noticed that there was a risk of fraud with prescription forms going missing. This led to an increased chance of medication being fraudulently obtained at an obvious cost to the taxpayer. Following this observation, the NHS introduced increased guidance, reporting tools and even mentioned the risk of prescription fraud within the NHS Counter Fraud Authorities control strategy (NHS, 2018). While the exact cost of fraud is never fully known, at the time it was estimated that losses exceeded £1.29 billion a year (NHS: Counter Fraud Authority, 2018).

Since the introduction of electronic prescriptions to prescribe medication, reducing the availability of prescription forms, the losses are estimated to have reduced to £1.198 billion (NHS: Counter Fraud Authority, 2022). This is a clear example of target removal. By utilising a technology-based solution, the NHS removed the ability for would-be fraudsters to commit the offence.

REDUCING THE MEANS

Reducing the means refers to reducing the enablers for the offender to commit crime. Often you see advice for homeowners to remove ladders from the front of their address or clear up rubble. The reason for this is to prevent giving the would-be burglars the means to get into your address whether that would be smashing the window with a brick or climbing through an open window on the first floor. This principle targets both the opportunistic offender who sees an opportunity and those who develop a successful MO over time. By spreading the message of how offenders commit this offence we reduce the availability of them doing so. Equally, this messaging needs to be balanced with the risk of highlighting vulnerabilities in addresses. Some criminals are opportunistic and by showing the public a risk we are also highlighting to them an opportunity.

REDUCING THE PAYOFF

Reducing the payoff means reducing the profitability of the offence meaning it is less worthwhile for the offender to commit. A common example is property marking. In the UK, the most popular scheme advertising this is Immobilise. This website sells products to assist with marking but also has a database where people can record the details of their high value items. Therefore, if they report an item as stolen, they can tell the police or update the national database themselves. This database can then be checked by the police when they seize an item or by resellers to check whether the item has been stolen (Recipero, 2022). This reduces the payoff by making some items unsellable through traditional methods such as second-hand shops who check the database to prevent having any losses themselves.

POLICING SPOTLIGHT

PC Green works for the BTP. At one of the stations in their area, a bike rack just outside the station building was regularly targeted by bike thieves. This has resulted in a large number of thefts being recorded and, as a result, PC Green was given some time to reduce these thefts alongside the train operating company (TOC) who funded the improvements.

Following a conversation with the TOC, PC Green managed to get improved CCTV installed in the area. This both improved the quality of the recording and meant that it can be remotely monitored by a 24/7 control room who in turn can alert the police if a deployment was required. New bike racks were installed that are more secure and signage about bike thefts had been put up. PC Green also ran a number of bike marking events at the station to talk to the public about thefts and help them mark their bikes so they can register them online.

CRITICAL THINKING ACTIVITY 6.1

LEVEL 4

Consider the bike marking above.

- What factors impact this intervention? Consider both the idea itself and the practicalities of implementing it.

- How can these be worked around?

- Do the marking events just reduce the payoff or are there other impacts that fit in with any other principles?

ACCESS CONTROL

Access control links directly to target hardening in that if people cannot gain access to what they want they cannot commit the offence. It is quite easy with this just to think in the physical sense; however, this can also be applied to digital crimes with the use of firewalls, passwords or encryption preventing access to data. Access control can sometimes be one of the easiest principles to address. Most places where an offence takes place have some sort of access that can be altered in some way to minimise access to those with criminal intent. However, this only tends to work on individual targets. If there is an issue in a wider area, this can be a little more troublesome.

You may have seen more recently an increasing use of access control when it comes to vehicles and crowded spaces. Over a few years, we have seen terrorist organisations and lone actors use a vehicle as a weapon, charging it into groups of people. As a result, in city centres and other areas barriers, planters or other obstacles are placed across the road, limiting vehicular access to only those who have permission.

SURVEILLANCE

Surveillance increases the risk of being seen and caught, both of which are off-putting to a would-be offender. Surveillance is typically associated with CCTV; however, in reality, it is much broader. For example, you could put a security guard in place or move the intended target to somewhere that will be seen more routinely in an attempt to increase natural surveillance.

Natural surveillances impact is based upon the availability of an audience, its alertness and the probability some action will come about following them seeing something happen (Jacobs and Cherbonneau, 2019). As police officers or prospective officers, I would suggest that you can understand that the desire of a criminal to commit an offence outside a police station at shift handover time would be low compared with committing it in a dark alleyway behind a business that is closed, and the reasons are obvious. Jacobs and Cherbonneau (2019) highlight three factors to consider when it comes to natural surveillance.

1. Isolation – victim-based crimes that take place solely with the victim present are far less likely to be caught than those in front of an audience.

2. Speed – this relates to the ability of the observers to be able to notice what is happening and act upon it. For example, in regards to carjacking, even when natural surveillance is high and people will see and understand what is happening, the audience's ability to act before it is too late is diminished if there is nothing to slow a potential escape.

3. Audience indifference – the article refers to the public not feeling an association with the victim, whether that be due to the makeup of the people in the locality or the fact that, as it did not affect them, they did not have the motivation to get involved.

CRITICAL THINKING ACTIVITY 6.2

LEVEL 5

- Using the above three factors consider how you as a police officer might influence these factors.

- Do you think this is something you can easily influence or is it better influenced by others? If so, who?

- Consider a public location local to you. Are there any reasonable changes that could be made to improve natural surveillance?

The other more commonly discussed form of surveillance is CCTV. One meta-analysis into CCTV's impact on crime has shown that across 76 different studies, on average, crime decreased by 13 per cent in the areas it is used. If this is broken down to locations where the CCTV was examined, housing areas were in line with the average, reporting an approximate decrease in crime of 12 per cent. However, the average increased to 37 per cent in studies where car parks were targeted (Piza et al, 2019). This highlights the value of surveillance. Typically, car parks are locations where natural surveillance is low. Consider how many times you have stayed in a car park for longer than required. CCTV fills the void where natural surveillance does not exist.

One popular example of increasing surveillance is through Neighbourhood Watch schemes. The schemes seek to reduce crime by increasing community cohesion, encourage interventions with neighbours and enable the flow of useful information from residents to policing thus increasing the chances of offenders being detected. Bennett et al (2008) reviewed the effectiveness of such schemes. This study did not find a reduction in crime; however, as it was limited, they used data from other research into Neighbourhood Watch schemes and excluded studies that did not allow them to review a percentage improvement themselves. This meant that just under half of the data obtained and reviewed by them was not able to be used in their crime reduction calculation. The authors also argue that the Neighbourhood Watch scheme may also increase crime statistics due to increased reporting and would-be offenders noticing that the area might have something worth protecting and as such worth stealing, again increasing crime. The same study also noticed that Neighbourhood Watches were far more likely to be successful in the USA and Canada rather than the UK. This could be due to the different neighbourhood dynamics seen in each country. Another study on

Neighbourhood Watch schemes in rural areas of the UK noticed that policing did not engage with Neighbourhood Watches frequently and only did so when there was a need. This meant that only 47 per cent of respondents to their survey felt Neighbourhood Watch increased community spirit. Despite that, there was a greater feeling of security and improved relations between residents and the police (Yarwood and Edwards, 1995). Therefore, while the empirical data might not support Neighbourhood Watches, the rise in crime could be an indication of its success and there are other benefits that other schemes do not provide such as increased connectivity to policing and increased community cohesion.

ENVIRONMENTAL CHANGE

Environmental change links back to the thinking behind broken windows theory and advocates the clearing of graffiti, ensuring the local amenities are in good working order and reducing the areas that naturally encourage crime to take place.

Street lighting is often a highly referenced improvement. However, one study in Wandsworth, London reported that improved street lighting did not have a significant effect on crime taking place. What it did improve was the attitudes of the residents, many citing increased perception of safety when walking at night (Atkins et al, 1991). The lack of impact on crime has been replicated worldwide with another study in Houston finding little link between the density of street lighting and crime, other than in one scenario where there was a much higher density of lights. The researchers, however, stated that this was probably due to increased footfall in the area justifying the lighting and it could therefore be because of increased natural surveillance (O'Connell, 2017).

RULE SETTING

Rule setting aims to set about new habits and change behaviours through the introduction of rules and positioning of signage to reinforce these rules. One such example you will see is at airports. There are endless restrictions on what can and cannot be taken on a plane and these have evolved over time dependent on the risk and the technologies available. We have also seen these rules evolve as the risk changes, such as searches and removal of shoes at security following the attempt by Richard Reid to blow up a plane mid-flight utilising an explosive concealed in his shoe (Hastings and Chan, 2013).

INCREASING THE CHANCES OF BEING CAUGHT

The principle of increasing the chances of being caught, when utilised in the real world, often can be seen to show other principles in action such as target hardening or improving surveillance. In the discussion about natural surveillance earlier one of the key factors was speed, and that the ability for an offender to escape was slowed down. This could be considered again as a means to improving the chances of being caught and measures taken slowing down the escape, therefore allowing a quicker policing response. Another example is the use of Smartwater. This is water-based liquid that has a unique system of being linkable to the location it was used and is only visible under UV light meaning offenders may not know where it was used (Smartwater, 2020). This increases the chances of being caught by providing law enforcement with additional opportunities to link an offence to an offender such as scanning potential suspects under a UV light. If Smartwater is suspected, then a sample can be taken and it can be linked to a potential scene or deployment of the water. We can also see, from the example below, increasing the chances of being caught can take a number of other steps.

EVIDENCE-BASED POLICING

THE SHOPLIFTING EXPERIMENT

A study in 1991 (Farrington et al, 1993) sought to establish the effectiveness of various crime prevention methods in preventing shoplifting in the Dixons store chain (Dixons was an electronics company similar to today's Currys). The three methods assessed were electronic tagging, store redesign and uniformed guards. The electronic tagging and security guard sought to increase the chances of being caught or at least the perception of this. The store redesign intended to decrease the opportunities for shoplifters by making it more difficult to commit the crime.

To ensure shoplifting was measured effectively, certain items in the stores had a label attached to them. Every time an item was sold the sticker was recovered and added to a tally and, prior to the day starting, all items with stickers were counted so an accurate stock count was known. Any number taken throughout the day would be noticed when the remaining stock on the shelves was counted at the end of the day.

In one store, it was identified pre-experiment that approximately 36.5 per cent of one of the items measured was being stolen by shoplifting. Post-experiment, having been subject to the redesign, 15.2 per cent of the same items was being stolen. The study also noted that electronic tagging significantly decreased shoplifting and the store continued to experience a decrease in thefts following the experiment indicating a residual effect post the intervention being used. Conversely, when reviewing the use of security guards, they had no significant effect on shoplifting in either store they were used in.

Despite having an impact, store tagging was not without its flaws. One store in the study reported that they were too short staffed to be able to respond to the alarm and also the stickers used to tag were found removed elsewhere in the store by the thieves. Equally, store redesign had its issues. For example, for it to be effective, standards must be maintained that post-test was seen not to be the case, albeit some elements remained, such as increased signage regarding the CCTV.

DEFLECTING OFFENDERS

Deflecting offenders is quite a broad area as it can mean that you take steps to deflect people away from thinking the target is suitable, such as using timers to switch on lights, or take steps to divert offenders through diversionary schemes.

A lot has been written about youth interventions, as diversion of young people from crime, which is often seen as a priority for governments. Hobson et al (2018) reviewed the effectiveness of a police-led project in Gloucestershire, which targeted those deemed at risk of offending by seeking to provide positive role models. Although the measurement of crime prevented is difficult, the study did identify a good link to the reduction of crime with those involved. In addition, the project rewarded those that engaged with the community through volunteering projects, which not only benefited the wider community but also sought to improve the individual's sense of value in the community. When the researchers costed the savings of the believed reduced crime and the impact of volunteering, it transpired that the initial investment of £321,000 actually provided a net saving overall.

Diversion programmes are not just for young people. For example, there are mental health adult interventions, many of which are based in a custody environment. They seek to divert individuals away from the criminal justice route by conducting early assessments and referring people to the correct support where required. One study noticed that a large majority of those people diverted would not otherwise have been referred for mental health treatment and 31 per cent of those who were referred ended up being admitted to a psychiatric hospital (Wood et al, 2011).

DIFFERENT TYPES OF CRIME PREVENTION

These principles are key ideas to remember when thinking about potential crime prevention interventions in your role. Interventions do not have to be as elaborate as some of the studies have shown and can just be about providing the right level of advice to the right person using the principles as a guide.

When it comes to more formal approaches to crime prevention intervention, there are two key approaches used. These are situational crime prevention and CPTED.

SITUATIONAL CRIME PREVENTION

The College of Policing (2022c) states that situational crime prevention aims: *'to increase risk and/or minimise reward, thus making either the commission of a criminal act too difficult, or the reward for committing the act too low to risk being caught'*.

104 CRIMINOLOGY AND CRIME PREVENTION

If we are to use the principles, this means that the crime prevention methods taken intend to either target harden potential targets or reduce the payoff and do so by individually examining the specific issue and coming up with tailored solutions.

To help assist with this, Cornish and Clarke (2003) created 25 techniques for situational crime prevention, organised into five key areas, which is seen in Table 6.1.

Table 6.1 Twenty-five techniques of situational prevention

Increase the effort	Increase the risks	Reduce the rewards	Reduce provocation	Remove excuses
Target harden	Extend guardianship	Conceal targets	Reduce frustrations and stress	Set rules
Control access to facilities	Assist natural surveillance	Remove targets	Avoid disputes	Post instructions
Screen exits	Reduce anonymity	Identify property	Reduce emotional arousal	Alert conscience
Deflect offenders	Utilise place managers	Disrupt markets	Neutralise peer pressure	Assist compliance
Control tools/ weapons	Strengthen formal surveillance	Deny benefits	Discourage imitation	Control drugs and alcohol

Cornish and Clarke, 2003

You can see from Table 6.1 that much of the principles' wording is reused; however, they should be seen in a different context. The benefit of the table is that you are able to look at your specific crime problem and then consider whether any of these options can be utilised to help make the offence harder or reduce its payoff.

POLICING SPOTLIGHT

PC Cox works for the venue licensing team for your police force. A particular venue is having an issue with sexual assaults taking place inside the toilets at the venue.

Using Table 6.1, PC Cox sat down with the licence holder and, having considered their options, decided to do several things.

To deflect the offenders, rather than having unisex bathrooms the venue redesigned them to separate both males and females at opposite sides of the bars. To reduce anonymity, ID scanning software was introduced, which was to be used upon entry to the venue for all patrons. The venue also agreed to increase the guardianship by having one or two extra door staff in and around the toilets at key times. To help alert the public's awareness of the issue, a number of posters were put up reminding people about the issue of consent and also information relevant to the VAWG strategy.

REFLECTIVE PRACTICE 6.2

LEVEL 5

- Reflecting on the above and the table of techniques are there any other steps you would take?

- Are there any actions taken that you do not feel would be impactful and, if so, why?

- Do you think the table assists in helping produce solutions?

- Have a look at your force website. What steps are they taking to reduce crime in the night-time economy?

CPTED

The other common approach to crime prevention is through environmental design. This approach looks more directly at the environment in which incidents take place and seeks to make alterations to improve public safety and reduce fear (College of Policing, 2022d).

Proponents argue that six component parts make up the approach to CPTED and that by addressing each one in turn we take steps to make a location safer (Figure 6.1). Some of these factors have already been discussed earlier in the chapter so to prevent repetition are not discussed here.

Figure 6.1 The component parts of CPTED

TERRITORIALITY

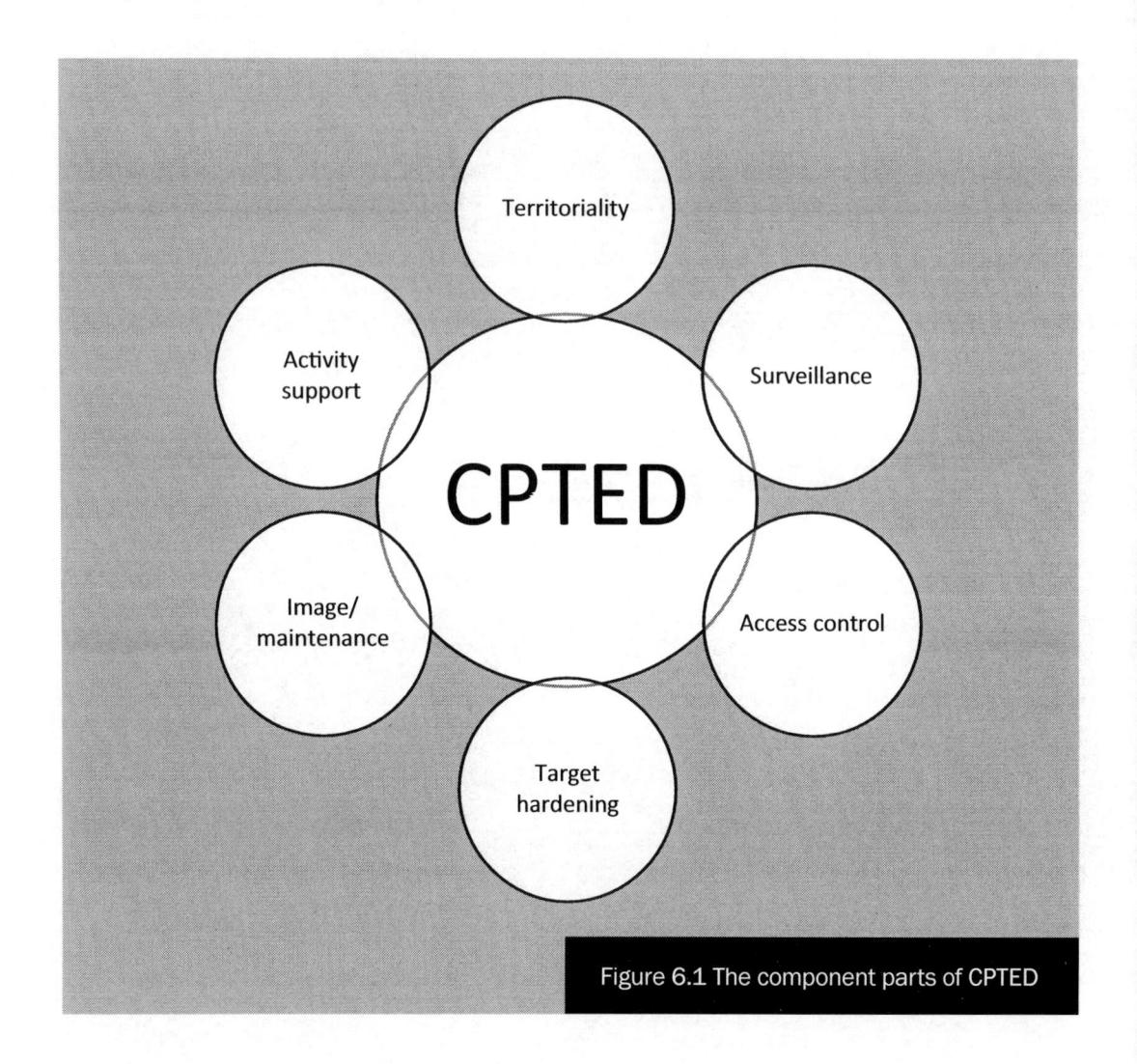

Territoriality relates to the idea of creating a sense of individual concern for the areas they live in. This sense of ownership means that those that reside there are less likely to allow those who are engaged in illicit activities to come in.

IMAGE AND MAINTENANCE

Image and maintenance relate to promoting a positive image of the area and allows the area to function seamlessly. Such an example will be to ensure places do not look abandoned to prevent people with criminal intent congregating there. This is broken windows theory in action.

When it comes to image, there is less research in that area, However, one article argued that vegetation might help reduce crime, while excessive amounts foster fear of crime and allow for hiding places for criminals. The right level, however, might encourage surveillance through encouraging people to use the spaces, act as a good marker for territorial behaviours and mitigate violence through reducing the psychological precursors. The study noticed that areas with high levels of vegetation had 52 per cent fewer crimes, and 56 per cent fewer violent crimes (Kuo and Sullivan, 2001).

ACTIVITY SUPPORT

Activity support relates to the signage and encouragement or discouragement of certain activities that can inhibit or encourage crime to take place. An example can be to encourage people to attend a social event, which will increase natural surveillance. Equally you may have seen signs in an area encouraging you not to do a certain act such as littering. Both are examples of this in action (Cozens et al, 2005).

KNOWING WHAT WORKS

Crime prevention is a challenging task. It is hard to know what works and even when an intervention is implemented, it is hard to know what would have taken place if the intervention was not there. As a result, it is important to know what works and how following implementation of a strategy you measure success.

When designing and implementing an intervention, cost is important. An effective way of being able to rationalise that cost is a good and well thought out review. While this book does not intend to be a guide on how best to conduct evaluations, it does help policing going forward if evaluations are shared and detailed. Afterall, you would not want to waste money on an intervention, which if properly evaluated, you would have known that it would have never worked in the first place. Evaluations are often expensive to conduct, especially if sample sizes are large enough to be effective and research is conducted over a long enough period to show sustained effects (Fagan and Buchanan, 2016). However, the positive implications across the service of an effective review make them worthwhile and, on occasion, costs can be mitigated using university students keen to undertake research.

Barry Poyner (1993) conducted a review of evaluations on crime prevention interventions and noticed that a number of them had some flaws in their examination. For example, often articles would claim a reduction in crime; however, on occasion, the reductions were not statistically significant, or their methodology was such that it could not be followed.

He also highlighted that claiming crime had been reduced was quite broad. Interventions are usually targeted at a specific crime type and, as a result, success should be measured using those crime types. Equally, by claiming that a change in bus pricing, for example, just influenced one crime type is too narrow. It should be worth noting that such examples were rare and, in his review, often crime prevention research was academically sound. These lessons are important to remember when you do your own research and projects. You do not want a highly successful project not be given the credit it deserves due to a poor evaluation.

To help assist in your own practice, a range of public and private agencies have created lists on what works, and an American version of such a database can be found on the website https://crimesolutions.ojp.gov. In the UK, the College of Policing has the What Works Centre for Crime Prevention, which is part of a network of 13 centres providing the public sector with the evidence to help utilise evidence-based solutions. This is a really helpful resource for your practice and includes a crime reduction toolkit that measures the effectiveness of interventions. It has a research map so you can see what areas of crime reduction work are being reviewed to prevent duplication and it also provides guides on a range of policing matters (College of Policing, ndb).

WHERE DOES CRIMINOLOGY FIT IN?

Having read this chapter, you might wonder how criminology threads its way through crime prevention, especially when the research mentioned in the chapter seems to have no criminological basis whatsoever. However, you will notice from Chapter 2 that the causes of offending are directly challenged by some of these interventions.

In CPTED, we have seen elements of broken windows theory in both showing that people care and challenging behaviours. By actively looking after the environment, we will naturally raise the thresholds that people expect and act upon.

Most interventions, however, seemingly interact and utilise rational choice theory. If criminal decision making is a weighing scale as described, then most interventions try their best to heavily skew the balance against offending. With the principles of crime prevention, the use of rational choice theory goes much deeper. We can see with the increase in surveillance, rule setting and increasing the chances of being caught directly interplay with the idea of general deterrence.

Specific deterrence, where we focus on the individual and their future behaviours, is seen directly in the principles when we reduce the payoff and deflect offenders. You have read, for example, about a scheme in Gloucestershire that aimed to not only divert those most at risk of committing crime towards positive activities, but also instil in them a sense of community spirit to make them reconsider their actions in the future.

In relation to routine activity theory, crime prevention actively interacts with the crime triangle to reduce offending and you can see in Cornish and Clarke's (2003) 25 situational crime prevention methods that, in some way, each one attacks at least one side of the triangle to dissuade potential offenders.

Finally, distance decay theory argues that both distance and a range of factors interact to mean that crime becomes more difficult to commit the further away from an offender's home. Crime prevention seeks to utilise this to add a number of factors to make crime harder. For example, access limitation to a block of flats limits the offender's ability to commit a crime; or events within a neighbourhood would mean that the offender sticks out to the residents more than they otherwise would.

SUMMARY OF KEY CONCEPTS

This chapter has explored the interesting approaches to crime prevention.

- There are 10 principles of crime prevention, which will ensure effective implementation in relation to a crime prevention challenge.

- Natural surveillance is the concept that surveillance is more than just CCTV and people also have an impact.

- Deflecting offenders has shown a net saving in the research conducted around youth programmes.

- There are 25 techniques for situational crime prevention, which can be helpful when addressing a problem.

- CPTED looks at how the environment interacts with crime with five key factors to make crime more difficult.

- Crime prevention should not be seen in isolation and has been seen to interact with criminological theory. Elements of broken windows theory, routine activity theory and the distance decay model can be seen in a large majority of examples.

CHECK YOUR KNOWLEDGE

1. Can you name the 10 principles of crime prevention?

2. How could you evaluate a crime prevention strategy to know what works?

3. How effective is street lighting at deterring crime?

4. What is an example of reducing the means to commit an offence?

5. What does 'reducing the means' mean?

Sample answers are provided at the end of this book.

FURTHER READING

College of Policing (2022) Response – Developing New Homicide Prevention Initiatives. 19 October 2022. [online] Available at: www.college.police.uk/guidance/homicide-problem-solving-guide/response-developing-new-initiatives.
This details the College's suggestions regarding situational crime prevention in regards to the increase in violent crime and homicides. What is helpful is that you can see the application of the 25 methods of situational crime prevention and the College provides suggestions for each relevant point. If you find the concept a bit abstract, this will be helpful to you to put it all into a practical example.

Recipero (2022) About the Immobilise System. [online] Available at: www.immobilise.com/about.
This is a helpful website to promote and be aware of while policing, especially if you are in a community policing role. The services and products are ideal and relatively inexpensive items that you can encourage members of the public to purchase or, if you have been given funding, you could also use. Its effectiveness is also reliant on policing and second-hand resellers utilising the National Mobile Property Register (NMPR).

Neighbourhood Watch (2020) Home Page. [online] Available at: https://ourwatch.org.uk.
Earlier in this chapter, there was a discussion about Neighbourhood Watch and its effectiveness. At times it is an underused resource. Consequently, it is well worth being aware of what areas they cover and what kind of activities they could do. If budget or time is tight, you might find that community action is a viable alternative.

CHAPTER 7
POLICING APPROACHES

LEARNING OBJECTIVES

AFTER READING THIS CHAPTER YOU WILL BE ABLE TO:

- understand hot spot policing, problem-oriented policing, intelligence-led policing and community policing;

- illustrate how to apply these various policing approaches in the real world;

- compare each method understanding their pitfalls and benefits.

INTRODUCTION

There is no one size fits all model to policing and there are several methodologies we will explore that you can use to police the area you work in, beyond that of just responding to calls whether that be in a neighbourhood role, as an investigator or even as an offender manager. The approaches covered in this chapter can be used in isolation or as a combination with each other. The first three approaches are much more focused towards tackling the problems policing faces. Community policing, however, is a far broader approach, which utilises a bit of all the models but does so with the community at the centre. At the end of the chapter, there is an example to allow you to apply the methodologies in practice.

HOT SPOT POLICING

If you work in response or neighbourhood policing, you may come across several crime maps and as you review them you should begin to notice areas of interest. When I was being taught how to police, my tutor referred to using such information as 'making your own luck'. At a basic level this is hot spot policing, and research has allowed policing to refine it and make it more effective.

In 1989, Sherman et al conducted one of the first studies looking at hot spot policing. They found that over half of police calls were dispatched to just 3.3 per cent of all addresses and intersections in the area. In relation to predatory crime such as sexual offences, they noticed that if one place had three of these offences the chances of reoccurrence in the same place was over 50 per cent, whereas the rest of the city generally only had an 8 per cent chance of those offences taking place. By knowing this, does it make sense to randomly police our areas or rather, especially when resourcing is tough, to target these most likely areas and increase the policing impact?

REFLECTIVE PRACTICE 7.1

LEVEL 5

Think about a time where you have been patrolling.

- What kind of areas did you go to?

> - Why did you attend these areas?
>
> - When you went to these areas were you looking for anything in particular?
>
> If you are not at that stage yet, think about a local area and think what type of crime takes place there and how you would patrol that area.
>
> - Now go onto the police.uk website and look at the crime map. Use the filters to select different offence types and see whether your patrols match up with where the offences are. How could you make your patrols more targeted?

Both routine activity theory and rational choice theory underpin this idea. In routine activity theory one of the key factors was an absence of capable guardian. By police being present in the hot spots at the right time we install a capable guardian. Regarding rational choice theory, by having police in these areas we increase both the fear and likelihood of being caught thus negatively impacting on the offenders' perceived chances of successfully committing an offence, which decreases their motivation to commit an offence.

Of course, officers cannot spend all their time in hot spots. Koper (1995) conducted one study, which not just looked at the effectiveness of hot spot policing but also whether the effectiveness was impacted by the length of their stay. The study utilised observers in hot spot areas of a city, measuring not just crimes and police presence but also other forms of disorder such as drunkenness. The study's concern regarding longer police presence was that with a longer police presence the impact might not move criminality from the area or make offenders more cautious. But rather the police presence becomes normalised, in which case does the residual effect of officers having been in an area diminish if officers are there too long? The study found that for every minute in a hot spot area, it increased the positive effects of the police presence. However, it did find that often the presence was in response to disorder reported thus meaning their attendance was always going to have some positive impact. In relation to length of time spent in an area, however, the positive effects reached a plateau between 14 and 15 minutes, meaning that any time spent beyond that period did not return a benefit on investment.

The College of Policing conducted a meta-analysis (an analysis that looks at a lot of other research and cuts it down to the important bits) on which types of crime hot spot policing impacts most. They found that it was most effective at reducing drug offences followed by disorder offences, property crime and then violent crime. All these crime types show a statistically significant impact when hot spot policing was used (College of Policing, 2018).

Policing is not just about police officers. Ariel et al (2016) researched whether PCSOs had a similar effectiveness to officers. It discovered that PCSOs did indeed have a positive impact on the reduction of crime. The study showed a 64.8 per cent decline in offences compared with the control groups but also found that PCSOs were able to provide a greater frequency of visits, most going over the requested three 15-minute visits a day. When doing their patrols, they were instructed to concentrate on being visible rather than conducting patrols to target a specific issue or problem solve.

EVIDENCE-BASED POLICING

In a study in St Louis, America, researchers alongside police used crime data to highlight 47 small geographic areas in the city with the highest frequency and concentration of firearm violence. These were narrowed down considering police policy and resourcing, meaning 32 areas were part of the trial. These were subsequently split into groups to evaluate what activity worked: normal policing, slow patrols with little self-initiated enforcement action and slow patrolling with a more proactive approach to enforcement.

Over the nine-month study, researchers showed an increased police presence in the requested hot spots and that, as requested, those in the third group of proactive enforcement were more proactive than in other areas. The result of this intervention meant that in the treatment areas firearm violence dropped by 43.7 per cent. For those that were less proactive, the average decrease was 45 per cent; however, in the areas where officers were more proactive, the resulting drop in crime was up to 63.8 per cent (Rosenfeld et al, 2014).

REFLECTIVE PRACTICE 7.2

LEVEL 4

Imagine you were a beat sergeant in an area that has a regular issue with robberies, which take place at two identifiable hotspots.

- How would you brief your team on how to actively use hot spot policing without it having too much of a drain on your resourcing?

CONCERNS WITH HOT SPOT POLICING

RESPONSE TIMES

A key performance measurement in policing is response times. In one recent study, practitioners argued that if officers were spending time at a certain location and were encouraged to get out of the car, their ability to respond and do other important work would be reduced. Despite that, however, the study found that because of the nature of why hot spots gained their status, in most cases the response times actually decreased and in the one area it did increase it was by only by a small amount, meaning their response time was still better than other areas (Telep et al, 2012).

CRIME DISPLACEMENT

Crime is seen by some as fluid and, because of this, crime will always happen somewhere. Based on that, there is an argument that by focusing our efforts on one area it is likely that we will just move crime somewhere else or displace it. Criminologically, it makes sense for crime to be displaced to other areas without a suitable guardian as some people will still have their motivation to offend. Crime, however, is more complex than that. While these areas might be soft targets, there are also other factors that encourage them to be hot spots. Whether that is being at a crossroads or an area where people naturally congregate, as a result, if there is not a natural secondary location where these other factors combine, the offending may cease. In the study involving PCSOs and hot spot policing the opposite was noticed, which was named a 'diffusion effect' with the positive impacts of this tactic influencing the local area nearby with a reduction in crime (Ariel et al, 2016). On a practical level, this will make sense. Officers cannot just appear in an area by magic and as such, by regularly visiting certain areas frequently, you will also naturally patrol the areas around it.

The displacement factor, however, is something worth considering. If you have a crime analyst, this maybe something they can help with, especially if you are measuring the effectiveness of your intervention. I would argue that while you may have prevented it annoying one group of residents, moving it to another group or another beat does not mean you have solved the issue entirely.

PROBLEM-ORIENTED POLICING

Goldstein (1979) argued that often agencies become so preoccupied with running their organisations that they forget the primary purpose for which they were created. In his article, he stated that often the focus of organisations was the means that they go about their business, which are often highly measurable, such as response times, rather than the end goal of providing a quality service and reducing crime, and because of this on the conclusion of various projects we are often left questioning whether they achieved anything.

To flip this discussion on its head, it is argued that a more targeted approach to issues should be taken, aiming to solve them rather than put a measure on effectiveness, and the most common way of doing so is by utilising the SARA model:

- **s**canning;

- **a**nalysis;

- **r**esponse;

- **a**ssessment.

SCANNING

This involves assembling the evidence around what issue you are seeking to tackle. This would not just be crime data but could also be from housing, local businesses or what local residents tell you. The aim here is to collect as much relevant information as possible to allow the analysis to be complete.

ANALYSIS

In your analysis, you aim to identify the conditions that allow the problem to exist, focusing on the areas that you can practically influence. A straightforward way to ensure all options are covered is by looking at the crime triangle (Figure 7.1).

Figure 7.1 The crime triangle

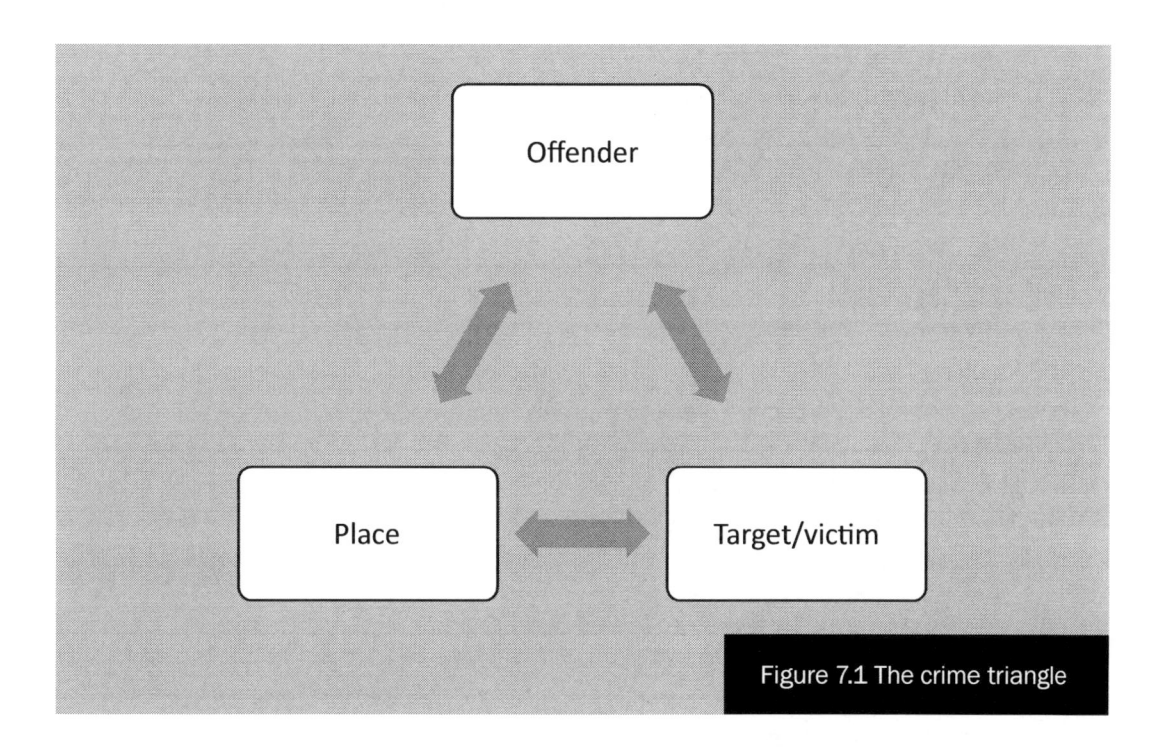

By reviewing all the factors influencing the crime triangle, a detailed picture of the issue can be established. This will allow targeted interventions, which might not be immediately obvious if you were just considering the crime data. When considering these factors, the ASU Center for Problem-Oriented Policing highlights that you should also be aware of those that have a stake in each side of the crime triangle, as influencing these key stakeholders will help improve the effectiveness of your intervention. They named these people: handlers for the offender, which are people who influence their behaviour (think the parents or guardians for a naughty child); places often have managers who take control of the environment (such as a shopping centre manager); and finally victims or targets often have guardians (ASU Center for Problem-Oriented Policing, nd). For an intervention to be effective, engagement with these individuals is essential and obtaining some buy in is the most effective means of ensuring progress. What is also evident is that to successfully utilise this style of policing we cannot rely on police-based information alone. Crime does not take place in a vacuum within society and, as a result, we should ensure our responses draw from as wide a range of sources as possible.

RESPONSE

Having completed your analysis, you should be able to identify some weak spots in the crime triangle, which can be targeted and consequentially action should be taken. While a triangle does not exist with one side removed, it is good practice to attempt more than one mitigation method in case one does not work or have the desired effect. When selecting your response, it is also important to be realistic. Unless policing has drastically changed in-between drafting this book and publication, policing as an example does not have the money to build a 5m-high wall around an estate. But what police might have influence with is the local housing agency or shops in the area.

ASSESSMENT

Once action is taken, it is important to assess the impact. It is possible that the actions taken have not had the desired effect or even had unintended consequences. When conducting the assessment, it is important to do so objectively and in line with what the original aims were and with an acceptance that sometimes you might have to go back to the drawing board. Again, crime statistics should not be solely relied on. It might be that those involved have evolved their behaviours into something that, while not criminal, might still be negatively influencing the community.

EVIDENCE-BASED POLICING

One study that tested the premise of problem-oriented policing was conducted by Eck and Spelman (1987) in an article that hopefully was inspired by *Ghostbusters* when it was entitled 'Who Ya Gonna Call?' Their study was based in Baltimore County, which had two murders within a week, which led to an understandably increased fear of violent crime.

As a result of this, a new department was established and, after an initial period where not much creativity was shown, they were trained in the theory and practice of problem solving. Officers began engaging in research such as speaking to residents about issues and engaged with other agencies. They then selected solutions and tested them to see whether they worked.

Such an example was the fear of street robberies in a local area. Following an analysis of the area, the officers identified that most of the residents were elderly, felt vulnerable and did not leave their apartments after dark. This was made worse by the condition of their local complex with poor lighting and poor maintenance of shrubs, which allowed offenders to conceal themselves.

As a result of this, the residents, alongside the police, formed a residents' association. They spread crime prevention advice and encouraged the local energy company to repair and replace lighting and other inspectors within the county visited the building to put pressure on the owner. This resulted in acquisitive crime dropping in the apartment complex.

CRITICAL THINKING ACTIVITY 7.1

LEVEL 4

Have a look at both problem-oriented policing and hot spot policing.

- What do you think the benefits of each are?

- What are the drawbacks to their implementation?

- Are there any issues that suit one style over the other?

Much like hot spot policing, the College of Policing have conducted a review into the effectiveness of problem-oriented policing. They found that interventions that focused on place managers, offenders or victims were not significantly different from one another and that combining it with hot spot policing was particularly effective. Interestingly, for all the examples that were based in England, all returned a total cost saving (College of Policing, 2017) compared with if crime was allowed to continue without intervention.

POLICING SPOTLIGHT

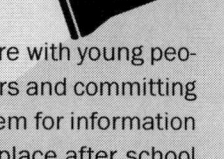

There is a regular issue with anti-social behaviour (ASB) in a town centre with young people in particular hanging around outside one store, harassing customers and committing low-level public order offences. The police officer scans the crime system for information and speaks to the local businesses who tell them the incidents take place after school hours but before 9pm. They also send a PCSO who has a good relationship with the young people to see why they congregate there. It transpires that the shop they are in front of has free Wi-Fi, which allows them to communicate with others without using their data. They also state that there is nothing for them to do and they go there as it is a focal point of the town and, as a result, if anything is going to happen, it is likely to be there.

In response to this, the officer speaks to the council who have arranged for a youth club to be set up nearby with activities to keep young people busy and the PCSO is deployed to promote it. In addition, the officer speaks to the store owner, who manages to get an IT engineer to move the Wi-Fi router further away from the entrance of the store, meaning it is harder for people to connect to it outside the building.

> Following several months, an assessment was conducted. There were still several young people in the area; however, the number was reduced, as was the number of incidents reported to the police. While the youth club was attended by a few people, it did not adequately entertain a few key individuals and as a result the activities were altered to better address their needs.

CONCERNS WITH PROBLEM-ORIENTED POLICING

POOR ANALYSIS

A common criticism is that the analysis given by policing is often cursory or non-existent. This might be a sign of pressures to get results or turn around quick solutions. But, more alarmingly, it is suggested that often the analysis was used to substantiate the existence of the suspected problem rather than build a meaningful insight. This approach could fundamentally undermine the effectiveness of this methodology and its main benefit of being able to suggest creative solutions. Bullock and Tilley (2009) argued that, unlike in health where this concept has been in action for some time and there is generally an agreed idea of what success is, within criminal justice there is no agreed hierarchy of evidence or key measurement that tells us what is effective, which makes research in this sphere so complex. This is one of the attractions of working in crime prevention. There is no black and white or clear-cut answer; however, it is also one of its biggest challenges especially when producing interventions or measuring their success.

NO ASSESSMENT OF IMPACT

This last letter in the SARA model is all about seeing whether something has worked. Cordner and Biebel (2005) noted that before and after comparisons are often omitted and utilisation of a control group is rare. In a world of social science and research, this is less than ideal. However, we must remember when conducting these assessments, we are not doing so in a lab space but are doing so within our local society and as such inaction, regardless of whether it is in the interests of science, is sometimes not an option. That said, before action is taken there should be some agreement about what success is. This allows everyone involved to know whether it is working.

The same article stated that police officers are more prone to action than research. This prevents an accurate understanding of the issue before interventions take place, limiting impact assessments. Evidence-based policing more recently is taking an increasing prominence in everyday work especially as it is advocated by the College of Policing and hopefully, over time, acceptance of research into what works will grow. Should you conduct your own study, do not let what is usually done hamper your ambition to try this approach if it is within the confines of your role and has the correct supervisory support.

LACK OF ENGAGEMENT

Problem-oriented policing by its very nature requires a number of stakeholders to be involved and, when creative solutions are found, often they are well outside the bounds of what the police can do. Consequently, without the correct level of support, progress will be limited. From personal experience when it comes to issues like this, it is important to understand what each party's motivation is to be involved in such a project. If we look at the earlier example outside the store, the shop's motivation is likely to be their customers and impact to business. If these are negatively impacted it becomes in their best interests to become involved. Engagement is often a longer-term requirement. Often when things are an issue people are more willing to engage. However, when it comes to the assessment of impact or even if the problem does not improve, interest can start to wane.

INTELLIGENCE-LED POLICING

Intelligence-led policing in some regards is like problem-oriented policing; however, it comes at the issue of crime from a slightly different approach. The main argument is that, rather than trying to address individual problems, you can reduce crime through proactive policing targeted by intelligence rather than the response-based approach that policing typically has towards crime. Rather than utilising the hot spot approach, intelligence-led policing is much broader and looks at ' *"hot people", "hot groups" and "hot places"* ' (Ratcliffe, 2016, p 64).

The origins of intelligence-led policing can be traced back to when financial constraints were a reality in policing. This also took place in an age where there was an explosion of available information on people and a thirst for more. As a result, there were two key reports in the UK that focused on effectiveness of policing but also providing value for money: the first being *Helping with Enquiries: Tackling Crime Effectively* (Audit Commission, 1993). This report was aimed at frontline policing and provided a user-friendly guide to cost-effective policing. The second report came from HMIC (now known as the HMICFRS), was titled 'Policing with Intelligence' and provided several key factors, which were required for the implementation of intelligence-led policing (Ratcliffe, 2002).

One of the pioneers of intelligence-led policing was Kent Police. Their approach in two police stations entailed a re-organisation of resources. Everyone's roles were aligned to a clear set of defined objectives with a focus on burglary and motor vehicle theft (Freilich, 2007, p 144). The main units were an intelligence cell, a tactical arrest team and a case preparation team with very few left in a reactive investigation team to deal with matters reported by the public. The intelligence cell played a key role in identifying priorities and these were relayed via a daily meeting with efforts made to target the most prolific offenders. Overall, within policing, it was seen as a positive with a strong impact on the key issues in the areas targeted. Victims of crimes not prioritised due to this targeted approach according to the research opted not to complain once it was explained why their crimes had not been investigated (Maguire, 2008, pp 453–4).

NATIONAL INTELLIGENCE MODEL

Intelligence-led policing follows the National Intelligence Model (NIM). The NIM provides a framework for information and intelligence to be passed through different points of the decision-making cycle, allowing it to influence strategic directions, the allocation of resources, tactical plans and tasking and co-ordination activity. To do so, it has three different levels, which focus on three different types of issues: level one being local, level two regional and force-level issues and, finally, level three, national, international and serious and organised crime (Keningale, 2020).

To assist with this, the NIM has highlighted the four core intelligence products which would help assist with this goal:

1. subject profile;

2. problem profile;

3. tactical assessment;

4. strategic assessment.

SUBJECT PROFILE

A subject profile aims to provide a comprehensive picture of a person, whether that be a victim, suspect or witness, and aims to provide their criminal history, lifestyle, associations and the risks they pose (College of Policing, 2019). By utilising this information to get ahead of the curve, police can be more proactive in their approaches and target areas known to be associated with the individual, meaning they are more impactful, lessening wasted efforts.

PROBLEM PROFILE

A problem profile is like a product you would expect when looking at an issue in regard to problem-oriented policing having conducted the analysis part of SARA. It seeks to not only identify the issues, but highlight the enablers, key players and key timings.

TACTICAL ASSESSMENT

A tactical assessment is a bit different from the previous two and is seen taking place at a supervisory level. It is used to identify the short-term issues for consideration by the tactical tasking and co-ordination group, define problems, identify subjects and trends, recommend tactical options, review intelligence requirements and review recent performance (College of Policing, 2019). From my personal experience especially at the lower levels, this usually takes the form of a meeting held at intervals and sets the direction for that area until the next meeting. When in practice I would recommend trying to find out what the priorities are for the area you are working in by taking steps in line with the tactical assessment in your everyday work. You are bound to make a name for yourself and produce results that are positively seen by supervisors.

STRATEGIC ASSESSMENT

This document is a more long-term assessment of likely issues but in some regards is much like the tactical assessments and is also influenced by priorities from other levels or external bodies (Maguire and John, 2006), such as, for an example, if there was a push from the Home Office regarding road safety. In my personal experience, these are often published yearly and have a few names such as a 'control strategy'. From reading this, you should have an idea of what issues are on the horizon for your area and potential mitigations in place. From a personal perspective, it is quite an interesting document to read and occasionally you will read about new things taking place in force before they are announced to staff.

CRITICAL THINKING ACTIVITY 7.2

LEVEL 5

Have a look online for the strategic assessment for the area you police or live in.

- What are the key priorities?

- What are the areas of risk?

- Does the plan provide any detail on the steps to be taken to tackle the problems?

Try looking at another force. It might be best to look at one that is within the 'most-similar group', a list of which is on the HMICFRS website.

- How do these reports contrast?

- Are there any similar threats for both areas?

- Why do you think the similar threats exist in both areas?

EVIDENCE-BASED POLICING

Operation Thumbs Down took place in Los Angeles and focused on a drug takedown operation targeting the 'Rollin' 30's Harlem Crips'. They were identified prior to the operation to be responsible for a considerable proportion of violence in the district. Prior to the operation, most agencies made an agreement to reduce gang violence; however, their impact had not really been measured prior to the operation. The FBI's (Federal Bureau of Investigation) approach centred on identifying the offenders and prosecuting where possible and therefore used both street-level enforcement and more complex approaches, such as the use of surveillance. Utilising the profiles identified above, this focused their efforts by targeting prolific offenders and groups utilising both tactical management and enforcement.

The implementation involved approximately 12 months of investigative work prior to a day of action on 29 August 2012, which resulted in 23 federal indictments, 18 state arrests and 16 federal arrests, and 24 federal and two state warrants being issued. As a result of this intelligence-led action, the research showed an approximate 22 per cent reduction in violent crimes (Ratcliffe et al, 2016).

ISSUES WITH INTELLIGENCE-LED POLICING

KNOWING WHAT IS OF USE

Intelligence understandably relies on information and assimilation of that information to transform it into a usable product. However, a key issue is to know what will be of use to law enforcement as its importance at the time of assimilation is often unknown. This results in policing trying to keep as much information as possible in case it becomes 'handy' (Ratcliffe, 2002), which then leads to making the good intelligence difficult to find and difficult to maximise among the noise.

IT CANNOT BE IMPLEMENTED IN ITS ENTIRETY

While the concept of intelligence-led policing is one of trying to get ahead of the curve of crime and tackling problems before they become too big of an issue, the reality is that a police force cannot become an entirely intelligence-led force. Policing is so complex today that while elements can be used, the public, however, still expect a service for certain crime types and in other cases, such as in domestic abuse, to effectively manage the risk a response-based service is required as well. While it is usable in the areas of policing that are measurable, the reality is that policing does not have access to vast amounts of data that could pre-empt crime. If we did, policing would be far more like *Minority Report*.

OVERSIMPLIFYING THE ROLE OF POLICING

If the role of policing were to simply cut crime, this model could be argued to be quite effective. However, in reality, policing is much broader than that. Even from a crime perspective, policing must do a lot of work just to tackle the fear of crime, which cannot be tackled by intelligence-led policing. In addition, policing is also involved in the search for missing people, assisting with mental health incidents and the policing of key events. These cannot be done with a purely targeted intelligence-led approach, albeit elements of it can be used.

COMMUNITY POLICING

Community policing is the most all-encompassing and broad policing style out of the four in this chapter and can in its very nature absorb parts of the previous three policing styles in its practice as it is more of a philosophical approach rather than a specific way of operation.

Cordner (2014) describes it as having three philosophical dimensions:

1. citizen input;

2. broad function;

3. personal service.

CITIZEN INPUT

Community policing puts a commitment on citizens to help decide on priorities and inputs. The premise behind this is that for policing to be effective they should have the support of those they police and therefore this input makes them both responsible and accountable. This can be seen to echo principle two of the policing principles set out by Sir Robert Peel in 1829 where he stated that the ability of the police to perform their duties is dependent on public approval of their actions. Sucic and Karlovic (2017) argue that collective efficacy (a collective desire for the same goal) requires a good level of social cohesion and that is shown to have an impact on crime rates and disorder. Consequentially, by police ensuring they have citizen input, we are encouraging all involved to be acting towards one goal.

BROAD FUNCTION

The police are not just there to fight crime but are there to enhance safety through tackling disputes, solving problems and preventing accidents. To narrow down the police's role to simply responding to incidents fails the public as to what they want most.

REFLECTIVE PRACTICE 7.3

LEVEL 4

Consider what is meant by 'broad function' and think about actions you expect a police officer to conduct or even actions you have taken when attending a scene and taking a crime report.

- On attendance, would you or the officer just take the details of the incident and then leave?

- What would you expect to happen that went beyond that?

- Is there anything else you could have done that would have helped towards this broad function goal?

PERSONAL SERVICE

The public do not want a generic service that is overly bureaucratic or one that shows that policing does not care about how the individual's crime has impacted them, other than just seeing them as just another victim statistic. Community policing seeks to redress this by making the police more accessible and contactable and personalising the experience by service users.

REFLECTIVE PRACTICE 7.4

LEVEL 5

Think about the above principles.

- Is there anything you could do in your practice that you think shows policing embracing community policing and why?

- Is there anything you think that goes against these principles? If they do, is there a reason as to why these principles have been side-lined?

- If you are not yet in service, think about the roles the public expect you to play. Is there any way you can alter your potential practice or response to crimes to help embrace community policing?

- Look online at your local police force. Do they promote anything that might be in line with community policing?

So why is community policing so important? We have seen from the Brixton riots (1981) and the subsequent Scarman report that engagement with communities is vital and that resorting to just basic policing methods can result in a degradation of the relationship with local people (Lord Scarman, 1981, pp 91–3). Engagement with people or the council acting on their behalf should lead to constructive conversations where people feel listened to and heard, as failure to do so can further add to frustration.

The Brixton riots is not the only time poor engagement has caused issues. If you have a chance, it may be worth having a review of the Macpherson report, which is another key review into policing in England. This report was published following the Stephen Lawrence murder and looked in the issues surrounding policing, including institutional racism and the effectiveness of the police investigation. What followed was a wide range of recommendations, which still impact on policing today. One of which was that policing needed to take steps to increase trust and confidence in sections of the community (Macpherson, 1999) and even 20 years on, it is still identified that policing needs to improve community engagement in policing (College of Policing, 2021a).

IMPLEMENTING COMMUNITY POLICING

Cordner (2014, pp 156–7) broke down the implementation of community policing into three key tactics:

1. positive interaction;
2. partnerships;
3. problem solving.

POSITIVE INTERACTION

Policing by its very nature can be confrontational. Even if you have not started your career yet, I am sure you can foresee at some point a member of the public not being overly happy with what you might have to do. Community policing seeks to redress that and balance the negative interactions with positive ones, such as crime prevention work or community engagement events. The aim for this is to increase familiarity with the public. This way they are more likely to give you information about what is happening in your area or be more accepting when something negative happens involving policing.

PARTNERSHIPS

The next element is partnerships. This is not just the formal partnerships policing has through partnership agencies but also those with citizens. Given the broad function that policing has, it is near impossible to be able to meet those objectives alone and as such fostering good and productive relationships with others goes a long way towards that.

CRITICAL THINKING ACTIVITY 7.3

LEVEL 4

Think about the range of partnerships that policing has, whether with voluntary organisations, statutory bodies or volunteers within the police themselves.

- What value do you think they add to policing?

- Do you think policing could absorb those roles within themselves?

    - If so, how?

    - If not, why not?

PROBLEM SOLVING

Much like intelligence-oriented policing, this takes a step away from typical response-based policing. It argues that, for community-based police to work when officers attend these incidents, they do not just try to deal with the immediate issue, but they take steps to prevent reoccurrence. This means that attendances are much more impactful and meaningful. Problem solving clearly draws influences from problem-oriented policing and many of its principles and approaches would be echoed in community policing work.

ISSUES WITH COMMUNITY POLICING

LACK OF ENGAGEMENT

While community policing aims to build bridges between the entire community in the area in which they operate, realistically there are some challenges. We have seen there are sections of the community that feel marginalised and disaffected and therefore, despite policing efforts, these groups have been slow to engage. In addition, it has been reported that those who do want to engage face intimidation from others within their community, therefore putting them off from engaging entirely. This clearly is a big barrier to the implementation of community policing. To make the impact it desires, it must find a way to effectively engage with these communities. Long term, if this is achieved, then the representational issues faced by the police workforce may also start to be addressed.

POOR STATUS WITHIN POLICING

Community officers by their very nature conduct a vastly different role to most other officers. As a consequence, they are not seen by their colleagues as 'real officers' and can be given disparaging names. This is not aided by their roles aimed at tackling more social issues. This internal struggle could mean that potentially good officers are put off from taking on that role, leading to skills drain, and efforts undertaken by those in that post are undermined by others who may not fully understand the benefits they bring. Moreover, due to the nature of policing, officers often must engage in activities that undermine the relationship with the community they are trying to foster, thus limiting its effectiveness (Tilley, 2008, pp 393–4).

From personal experience, community policing can be really rewarding. At times, you get successes that other officers do not due to previous engagement and a key benefit is that you are not always running around trying to meet demand. It gives you the freedom to conduct policing in a different way and, if you get the opportunity, I strongly recommend you embrace neighbourhood/community policing roles.

CRITICAL THINKING ACTIVITY 7.4

LEVEL 5

Consider what you feel about the state of policing today.

- Does the service utilise one of these policing approaches over the other?

- What elements do you see in policing today that highlight each approach?

- Which one do you think is most effective at delivering a good service?

- Do you think there are any practices that could be altered to utilise one of these approaches more to help make policing more effective?

POLICING SPOTLIGHT

There is a sergeant policing a small town, which doubles in size over the summer due to a thriving tourist industry. Local residents have approached them and raised concerns over two key issues. First, the fear of violent crime on a Friday and Saturday night down the main road where a number of pubs and clubs are based. Second, the increase in non-dwelling burglaries, which is subsequently impacting on businesses' profits, which are important during the winter when the town is quieter.

They review the crime system and see no particular spike in violent crimes but have noticed that one particular area is being hit with a high level of burglaries and that a particular car park also has a high number of thefts from motor vehicles, both of which frustratingly happen at approximately the same time and are on opposite sides of the town.

Owing to the busy summer period, many staff have been moved to cover more pressing issues across the force. As a result, the sergeant has two PCs, and a PCSO, and themself to deploy. The response team covering the area are also on minimum staffing. Owing to the issues being raised to the chief constable via a letter from one of the residents, an intelligence researcher has been freed up for a day to help.

The sergeant asks the researcher to create a problem profile on the non-dwelling burglaries. It identifies a potential offender who is currently managed by the Integrated Offender Management (IOM) Team and shows that, despite the buildings having alarms, none have gone off during the offences.

As a result, the sergeant tasks the PCSO to visit premises in the area targeted during the day. They provide crime prevention advice and review security. In the evening, the sergeant separates the officers to conduct patrols in the areas identified, focusing on being as visible as possible. They also liaise with the local council to see whether the car park can have improved CCTV and whether it can be monitored at key times.

REFLECTIVE PRACTICE 7.5

LEVEL 4

- In the above scenario is there anything that could have been done differently? What would you advise?

- Is there any information you would want to know more about?

- Consider the policing approaches discussed: which ones would you utilise most in this scenario?

SUMMARY OF KEY CONCEPTS

This chapter has discussed the many different policing approaches.

- Hot spot policing centres around the concept that if you target the areas with the highest levels of crime with high visibility policing, commission rates will drop.

- The most effective periods for conducting hot spot policing according to research is between 14 and 15 minutes at each hot spot and its effectiveness is not impacted significantly if conducted by officers or PCSOs.

- Hot spot policing, however, does draw some criticism as focusing resourcing in one location might mean that response times are impacted. In addition, if you focus resourcing in one place, there is an argument that crime might go elsewhere, which is known as displacement.

- Problem-oriented policing focuses on resolving individual issues and the SARA model is used to ensure that the issues are fully understood and then interventions are accurately assessed for their impact.

- When conducting your analysis of the issue, it is important to keep a broad perspective as ongoing issues do not take place due to one factor alone. As such, consider the crime triangle of: place, offender and victim.

- Problem-oriented policing is also not without its issues. Often analysis is poor when looking at issues. The impact of interventions is not detailed enough and, due to the nature of the approach, it requires support from others, which is not always forthcoming.

- Intelligence-led policing seeks to look at key areas of concern and uses intelligence to get ahead of the issue, utilising four key tools: subject profile, problem profile, tactical assessment and strategic assessment. These are done at distinct levels depending on the breadth of the issue, ensuring that local issues are not excluded due to national priorities overtaking.

- Intelligence-led policing has its flaws. For example, it cannot be implemented in its entirety, it gives the impression that priorities mean that other elements of policing can be dropped and, as with all intelligence, sometimes it is difficult to know what is helpful and what is not.

- Community-led policing in some ways is a hybrid of the previous three models. It has three main philosophies, which are: community input, personal service and a broad function. These can be implemented by using positive interactions, partnerships and problem solving.

- Community policing, however, relies on involvement from others and, if you are trying to engage with the public, it is only successful if they engage back. In addition, it is believed to hold a lower status within policing.

CHECK YOUR KNOWLEDGE

1. What factors influence the effectiveness of hot spot policing?

2. Regarding problem-oriented policing, what does SARA stand for?

3. What is a tactical profile in the intelligence-led policing model?

4. In community policing, what is the benefit of having a positive interaction with the community?

Sample answers are provided at the end of this book.

FURTHER READING

ASU Centre for Problem-Oriented Policing. [online] Available at: https://popcenter.asu.edu/. This is a helpful website when it comes to researching problem-oriented policing. It has guides on different crime types and provides broader information on the implementation of the model. Please remember, however, that it is US based so some interventions might not be completely applicable in the UK.

College of Policing (nd) Crime Reduction Toolkit. [online] Available at: www.college.police.uk/research/crime-reduction-toolkit.

The crime reduction toolkit is a helpful tool to use in your practice. The College, on your behalf, look at a wide range of academic material regarding specific interventions and distil them down to what you need to know to help you police. Furthermore, this resource is constantly being reviewed and is ever growing, meaning the information is often more up to date than research you may have available to you locally. When it comes to your studies, if you are researching a particular intervention, it is also very helpful in pointing you in the right direction for some more academic resources if you need them.

Newburn, T (ed) (2014) *Handbook of Policing*. Cullompton: Willan Publishing.

While this book is a bit older, if you are looking at the more academic side of policing, it is a useful resource to have and covers a broad range of topics, which are still relevant to policing. Unlike Tim Newburn's *Criminology* (2007), this title is not seen negatively by markers and is an authoritative resource.

Reisig, M and Kane, R (eds) (2019) *The Oxford Handbook of Police and Policing*. Oxford: Oxford University Press.

Again, this a more academic book, which covers a broad range of areas including a helpful chapter on problem-oriented policing. Like other Oxford Handbooks, this book appeals more to the academic than the practitioner, albeit it is helpful to your practice and your studies.

SAMPLE ANSWERS

In this section you will find all the answers to the 'Check your knowledge' questions. In addition, and where helpful, there are answers to some of the questions raised elsewhere in each chapter.

CHAPTER 1

CRITICAL THINKING ACTIVITY 1.2

For the relevant criteria, it is important to select a range of people to ensure one section of the community is not excluded. Some examples of areas you might have considered are the following:

- age;

- sex;

- ethnicity;

- postcodes;

- socio-economic backgrounds.

CHECK YOUR KNOWLEDGE

1. The CSEW seek to address the 'dark figure' of crime. This refers to crimes the police do not hear about because they are not reported to them. As a result, the British Crime Survey often has a higher level of offences recorded than police recorded crime. It, however, does not completely capture offending – as an example state-based or business victims are excluded.

2. A traumatic response to an event may foster behaviours that increase the risk of victimisation. Examples such as over thinking or avoidance behaviours may, in turn, mean the victim experiences further crimes.

3. Various factors have been shown to increase the risks of being a victim of crime. For example, in repeat cases reported to the MASH, 75 per cent had mental health issues and 40 per cent had links to drugs or alcohol. Personal circumstance can also be a factor, such as being a lone parent, single or divorced. Even an increased use of public transport raised the risk of becoming a victim.

4. Event dependency relates to the idea that having been burgled once, you are more likely to be victimised again. This is because a would-be offender is aware that the target has previously been successful and therefore it poses less of a risk to target it again.

5. There are three levels of RJ:

    i. local level for ASB and low-level crimes that can be resolved through community resolution;

    ii. more complex crimes where RJ can be run alongside or instead of the criminal justice process;

    iii. complex and sensitive cases, where RJ can only be conducted by experienced practitioners.

CHAPTER 2

CRITICAL THINKING ACTIVITY 2.2

Regarding this activity, policing options can at times be limited. However, policing often has the opportunity to have those honest conversations with people regarding their issues and put in place voluntary referrals or signpost people towards help. You might find during your policing practice how few people know where to go when they need help.

Policing also has the power to put in place out of court disposals when people commit offences, which can directly address issues such as drugs or alcohol misuse.

Some forces also can do drug testing for certain matters on arrest. If someone tests positive, they are obliged to attend drug rehabilitation assessment or an offence is committed.

These are a couple of examples, and you may have thought of others.

CHECK YOUR KNOWLEDGE

1. Adverse Childhood Experiences are stressful or traumatic events, which if witnessed as a child put you at an increased risk of health issues and committing crime.

2. Routine activity theory utilises the crime triangle and the three sides are:

i. offender with capacity to commit crime;

ii. suitable target/victim;

iii. absence of capable guardian protecting the victim/target.

3. Distance decay theory argues that people commit offences within a geographic framework, the biggest of which is distance. The further away, the greater the diminished chances of offending. It argues that other factors linked to distance such as transportation availability for the offender all combine and impact on the distances available to the potential offender.

4. Broken windows theory is based around the perception of people caring for the area. It argues that if visible signs of disorder go unchallenged, it breeds further disorder.

5. Locating an offender can be done in a number of ways utilising mobile phones, money enquiries or social media. Another common way is utilising their network of friends and family to help provide ideas of where they might be.

CHAPTER 3

CHECK YOUR KNOWLEDGE

1. Procedural justice is the concept that people feel they are being treated fairly and without bias against them.

2. The four main principles of procedural justice are:

    i. conversation with those involved to get their engagement with decision making before a decision is made;

    ii. the perception that the decision made is neutral;

    iii. you show dignity and respect to the individual involved;

    iv. demonstrating that the interaction has trustworthy motives.

3. Procedural justice is important to policing for a number of reasons. Firstly, we police by consent. This means that we have the public onside and we are held

accountable. Secondly, procedural justice means that the public understand and can empathise with our decision making. This has been shown to de-escalate conflict.

4. Implementation can be difficult for a number of reasons:

    - it requires concentration, which at times of tiredness and stress can be difficult;

    - people's perception of procedural justice differs from one person to another meaning there is no one size fits all solution.

CHAPTER 4

REFLECTIVE PRACTICE 4.1

The most recent and topical example of the idea of social control could be seen during the Covid-19 pandemic. There was a lot of messaging towards the wearing of masks and vaccinations to name two issues. You could see these being enforced via both informal and formal methods of control.

CHECK YOUR KNOWLEDGE

1. The hierarchy of courts is the order in which trials progress through the CJS. At the start of it is the Magistrates' courts, which deal with most matters. This is followed by the Crown Court, Court of Appeal and Supreme Court. This applies to criminal cases only and the civil and family courts have a different hierarchy.

2. Police, probation, prison service, education, social care and housing can be involved in MAPPA. You may also find locally there are some variances in this, and more people are involved.

3. The two tests are the evidential test and public interest test. The evidential test is whether there is a realistic prospect of conviction on the evidence provided to the CPS. The public interest test is used if the first test is passed and ensures that it is in the public interest to prosecute the individual.

4. Social control is the mechanism by which society ensures that people adhere to the social norms.

CHAPTER 5

CHECK YOUR KNOWLEDGE

1. The role of the PCC is to hold the chief constable to account. They set budgets, set policing priorities and establish effective partnerships.

2. Political sentiment influences how receptive government is towards elements of police reform. We have seen two examples where, dependent on the government needs and objectives, impacts upon what reforms are brought in. The Conservative government argued the police cannot be trusted and as such we saw a wealth of reforms in that area. The Labour government argued that they were tough on crime and as such focused on the 'what works' agenda.

3. Body-worn cameras record police interaction with the public. This ensures they are kept accountable by providing a record of what has taken place, supporting quick resolution of complaints and, in some ways, ensuring the police self-regulate their actions.

4. The HMICFRS are the inspectorate for policing. Consequently, their role is to ensure police conduct themselves in line with the established standards. They regularly review forces to see how they are progressing and allow a way to compare forces with one another.

CHAPTER 6

CHECK YOUR KNOWLEDGE

1. The 10 principles for crime prevention are:

    i. target hardening;

    ii. target removal;

    iii. reducing the means;

    iv. reducing the payoff;

    v. access control;

    vi. surveillance;

vii. environmental change;

viii. rule setting;

ix. increase the chances of being caught;

x. deflecting offenders.

2. There are several ways to check whether a crime prevention strategy has worked. Firstly, you could compare crime offending rates. You could also look at the cost of implementation compared with the impact seen. Another important element is how the intervention has made potential victims feel. Part of policing is making people feel safer.

3. Street lighting from studies is not seen to have an effective impact on crime taking place; however, it did increase individuals' perceptions of feeling safe.

4. Such examples include removing items from your front garden that could be used to aid an offender and so prevent burglary.

5. Reducing the means refers to limiting the enablers for the offender to commit the offence.

CHAPTER 7

CHECK YOUR KNOWLEDGE

1. Hot spot policing is influenced by a number of factors including;

    - time spent on scene;

    - activity of the officers present;

    - type of crime being targeted.

2. SARA stands for:

    - scanning;

    - analysis;

- response;

- assessment.

3. A tactical profile is used to identify issues for consideration at a supervisory level, identify trends, recommend tactical options and review intel requirements and performance.

4. Positive interaction is helpful because it brings in a good interaction when policing interactions are often negative. This brings in familiarity with the public, which means they are more likely to provide information or be more accepting when things go wrong.

REFERENCES

Action Fraud (2022) 'Friend in Need' Scams Costs Whatsapp Users £1.5 million. 18 July 2022. [online] Available at: www.actionfraud.police.uk/alert/friendinneed (accessed 9 October 2023).

Ali, A and Champion, N (2021) *More Harm than Good.* London: Criminal Justice Alliance.

Amir, M (1967) Victim Precipitated Forcible Rape. *The Journal of Criminal Law, Criminology, and Police Science*, 58(4): 493–502.

Aplin, R (2023) Independent Advisory Groups (IAG): Managing the Divide between Communities and Police in Knowledge Sharing and Understanding. *Journal of Intelligence, Conflict and Warfare*, 53(3): 216–20.

Archer, B and Ellison, G (2023) *Police Procedure and Evidence in the Criminal Justice System.* St Albans: Critical Publishing.

Ariel, B, Sutherland, A, Henstock, D, Young, J, Drover, P, Sykes, J, Megicks, S and Henderson, R (2017) 'Contagious Accountability': A Global Multisite Randomized Controlled Trial on the Effect of Police Body-Worn Cameras on Citizens' Complaints against the Police. *Criminal Justice and Behaviour*, 44(2): 293–316.

Ariel, B, Weinborn, C and Sherman, L W (2016) 'Soft' Police at Hot Spots – Do Police Community Support Officers Work? A Randomized Controlled Trial. *Journal of Experimental Criminology*, 12: 277–317.

Association of Police and Crime Commissioners (nd) Role of the PCC. [online] Available at: https://apccs.police.uk/role-of-the-pcc/# (accessed 9 October 2023).

ASU Center for Problem-Oriented Policing (nd) The Problem Analysis Triangle. [online] Available at: https://popcenter.asu.edu/content/problem-analysis-triangle-0 (accessed 9 October 2023).

Atkins, S, Husain, S and Storey, A (1991) *The Influence of Street Lighting on Crime and Fear of Crime.* London: Home Office.

Audit Commission (1993) *Helping with Enquiries: Tackling Crime Effectively (Police Paper No. 12).* London: Audit Commission.

Baird, V A (2001) Building Institutional Legitimacy: The Role of Procedural Justice. *Political Research Quarterly*, 54(2): 333–54.

REFERENCES

Baybutt, M, Hayton, P and Dooris, M (2009) Prisons in England and Wales: An Important Public Health Opportunity? In Douglas, J, Earle, S, Handsley, S, Jones, L J, Lloyd, C E and Spurr, S (eds) *A Reader in Promoting Public Health* (pp 134–42). London: Sage.

BBC News (2010) Rapist Who Murdered Mother and Girl Jailed for 32 Years. 5 February 2010. [online] Available at: http://news.bbc.co.uk/1/hi/scotland/glasgow_and_west/8499943.stm (accessed 9 October 2023).

BBC News (2011) Fiona Pilkington Officers Face Misconduct Proceedings. 24 May 2011. [online] Available at: www.bbc.co.uk/news/uk-england-leicestershire-13504618 (accessed 9 October 2023).

BBC News (2021) Sarah Everard: How Wayne Couzens Planned Her Murder. 30 September 2021. [online] Available at: www.bbc.co.uk/news/uk-58746108 (accessed 9 October 2023).

BBC News (2022) Ava White: Boy Who Killed Girl, 12, in Snapchat Row Gets Life. 11 July 2022. [online] Available at: www.bbc.co.uk/news/uk-england-merseyside-62119537 (accessed 9 October 2023).

Becker, H (1963) *Outsiders*. New York: Free Press.

Bennett, C (2007) Satisfying the Needs and Interests of Stakeholders. In Johnstone, G and Van Ness, D W (eds) *Handbook of Restorative Justice* (pp 247–64). Cullompton: Willan Publishing.

Bennett, T, Holloway, K and Farrington, D (2008) *The Effectiveness of Neighborhood Watch*. Oslo: The Campbell Collaboration.

Blakey, R (2017) *Library Briefing: Rehabilitation in Prisons*. London: House of Lords.

Brantingham, P L and Brantingham, P J (1975) Residential Burglary and Urban Form. *Urban Studies*, 12(3): 273–84.

British Transport Police (2021) *2020/21 Annual Report*. London: British Transport Police.

Brooker, C, Collinson, B and Sirdifield, C (2022) Improving Healthcare in Adult Probation Services: Learning from Youth Offending Teams. *Probation Journal*. [online] Available at: https://doi.org/10.1177/02645505211070088.

Budd, T, Collier, P, Mhlanga, B, Sharp, C and Weir, G (2005) *Levels of Self-Report Offending and Drug Use among Offenders: Findings from the Criminality Surveys*. London: Home Office.

Buker, H (2011) Formation of Self-Control: Gottfredson and Hirschi's General Theory of Crime and Beyond. *Aggression and Violent Behavior*, 16(3): 265–76.

Bullock, K and Tilley, N (2009) Evidence-Based Policing and Crime Reduction. *Policing: A Journal of Policy and Practice*, 3(4): 381–7.

Cabinet Office (2013) Legislative Process: Taking a Bill through Parliament. 20 February 2013. [online] Available at: www.gov.uk/guidance/legislative-process-taking-a-bill-through-parliament (accessed 9 October 2023).

Cambridge University Press (nd) Crime. [online] Available at: https://dictionary.cambridge.org/dictionary/english/crime (accessed 9 October 2023).

Canter, D and Youngs, D (2008) Geographical Offender Profiling: Origins and Principles. In Canter, D and Youngs, D (eds) *Principles of Geographical Offender Profiling* (pp 17–34). Abingdon: Routledge.

Canter, D V and Gregory, A (1994) Identifying the Residential Location of Rapists. *Journal of the Forensic Science Society*, 34(3): 169–75.

Canton, R, Hine, J and Welford, J (2011) *Outside Chances: Offender Learning in the Community*. Leicester: City and Guilds Centre for Skills Development.

Carrabine, E, Lee, M, Plummer, K, South, N and Cox, P (2009) *Criminology: A Sociological Introduction*. Abingdon: Routledge.

Chermak, S (1995) Image Control: How Police Affect the Presentation of Crime News. *American Journal of Police*, 14(2): 21–43.

Clarke, R V, Field, S and McGrath, G (1991) Target Hardening of Banks in Australia and Displacement of Robberies. *Security Journal*, 2(2): 84–90.

Cohen, L E and Felson, M (1979) Social Change and Crime Rate Trends: A Routine Activity Approach. *American Sociological Review*, 44: 588–608.

College of Policing (2013) Engagement. 23 October 2013. [online] Available at: www.college.police.uk/app/engagement-and-communication/engagement (accessed 9 October 2023).

College of Policing (2014) *Code of Ethics*. Ryton: College of Policing.

College of Policing (2017) Problem-Oriented Policing. 25 May 2017. [online] Available at: www.college.police.uk/research/crime-reduction-toolkit/problem-oriented-policing.

College of Policing (2018) Hot Spots Policing. 21 April 2018. [online] Available at: www.college.police.uk/research/crime-reduction-toolkit/hot-spots-policing (accessed 9 October 2023).

College of Policing (2019) Analysis Intelligence Products. 3 April 2019. [online] Available at: www.college.police.uk/app/intelligence-management/analysis/analysis-intelligence-products#national-intelligence-model-products (accessed 9 October 2023).

College of Policing (2021a) Macpherson Report: 22 Years On. 29 July 2021. [online] Available at: www.college.police.uk/article/macpherson-report-22-years-on (accessed 9 October 2023).

College of Policing (2021b) Communication. 18 November 2021. [online] Available at: www.college.police.uk/guidance/vulnerability-related-risks/communication (accessed 9 October 2023).

College of Policing (2022a) Stop and Search. 22 April 2022. [online] Available at: www.college.police.uk/app/stop-and-search/legal (accessed 9 October 2023).

College of Policing (2022b) Restorative Justice: Evidence Briefing. 18 January 2022. [online] Available at: www.college.police.uk/guidance/restorative-justice/evidence-briefing (accessed 9 October 2023).

College of Policing (2022c) What Is Situational Crime Prevention? 19 January 2022. [online] Available at: www.college.police.uk/guidance/neighbourhood-crime/what-situational-crime-prevention (accessed 9 October 2023).

College of Policing (2022d) Physical Environment Interventions. 18 March 2022. [online] Available at: www.college.police.uk/guidance/interventions-reduce-violence-against-women-and-girls-vawg-public-spaces/physical-environment-interventions (accessed 9 October 2023).

College of Policing (2023) Professional Profile: Police Constable. 31 January 2023. [online] Available at: https://profdev.college.police.uk/professional-profile/police-constable/ (accessed 9 October 2023).

College of Policing (nda) About Us. [online] Available at: www.college.police.uk/about (accessed 9 October 2023).

College of Policing (ndb) What Works Centre for Crime Reduction. [online] Available at: www.college.police.uk/research/what-works-centre-crime-reduction (accessed 9 October 2023).

College of Policing and NPCC (2021) Policing Violence against Women and Girls: National Framework for Delivery: Year 1. College of Policing.

Conservative Party (2010) Invitation to Join the Government of Britain. April. [online] Available at: https://general-election-2010.co.uk/2010-general-election-manifestos/Conservative-Party-Manifesto-2010.pdf (accessed 9 October 2023).

Cordner, G (2014) Community Policing. In Reisig, M D and Kane, R J (eds) *The Oxford Handbook of Police and Policing* (pp 148–71). Oxford: Oxford University Press.

Cordner, G and Biebel, E P (2005) Problem-Oriented Policing in Practice. *Criminology and Public Policy*, 4(2): 155–80.

Cornish, D B and Clarke, R V (2003) Opportunities, Precipitators and Criminal Decisions: A Reply to Wortley's Critique of Situational Crime Prevention. *Crime Prevention Studies*, 16: 41–96.

Courts and Tribunals Judiciary (2023) Structure of Courts and Tribunals System. [online] Available at: www.judiciary.uk/structure-of-courts-and-tribunals-system/ (accessed 9 October 2023).

Cozens, P M, Saville, G and Hillier, D (2005) Crime Prevention through Environmental Design (CPTED): A Review and Modern Bibliography. *Journal of Property Management*, 23(5): 328–56.

CPS (2018) The Code for Crown Prosecutors. 26 October 2018. [online] Available at: www.cps.gov.uk/publication/code-crown-prosecutors (accessed 9 October 2023).

CPS (2019) Restorative Justice. 24 September 2019. [online] Available at: www.cps.gov.uk/legal-guidance/restorative-justice (accessed 9 October 2023).

CPS (2022) About CPS. [online] Available at: www.cps.gov.uk/about-cps (accessed 9 October 2023).

Crawford, A (2008) Plural Policing in the UK: Policing beyond the Police. In Newburn, T (ed) *Handbook of Policing* (pp 147–81). Cullompton: Willan Publishing.

Danechi, S and Tunnicliffe, R (2021) *PCC Elections 2021*. London: House of Commons Library.

Davies, M, Croall, H and Tyrer, J (2005) *Criminal Justice: An Introduction to the Criminal Justice System in England and Wales*. Harlow: Pearson Education.

Decker, S H (1993) Exploring Victim–Offender Relationships in Homicide: The Role of Individual and Event Characteristics. *Justice Quarterly*, 10(4): 585–612.

Delisi, M (2013) Revisiting Lombroso. In Cullen, F T and Wilcox, P (eds) *The Oxford Handbook of Criminological Theory* (pp 5–21). Oxford: Oxford University Press.

Dignan, J (2005) *Understanding Victims and Restorative Justice.* Maidenhead: Open University Press.

Dixon, B (2020) Who Needs Critical Friends? Independent Advisory Groups in the Age of the Police and Crime Commissioner. *Policing: A Journal of Policy and Practice*, 14(3): 686–97.

Drakulich, K M and Crutchfield, R D (2013) The Role of Perceptions of the Police in Informal Social Control: Implications for the Racial Stratification of Crime and Control. *Social Problems*, 60(3): 383–407.

East Ayrshire Chief Officers Group (2011) MAPPA Significant Case Review: Thomas Bennie Smith. [online] Available at: www.east-ayrshire.gov.uk/Resources/PDF/M/MAPPA SignificantCaseReviewThomasBennieSmith.pdf (accessed 18 September 2023).

Eck, J E and Spelman, W (1987) Who Ya Gonna Call? The Police as Problem-Busters. *Crime and Delinquency*, 33(1): 31–52.

Ellingworth, D, Hope, T, Osborn, D R, Trickett, A and Pease, K (1997) Prior Victimisation and Crime Risk. *International Journal of Risk, Security and Crime Prevention*, 2(3): 201–14.

Elliott, C and Quinn, F (2007) *English Legal System.* Essex: Pearson.

Ellwood, C A (1912) Lombroso's Theory of Crime. *Journal of the American Institute of Criminal Law and Criminology*, 2: 716–23.

Fagan, A A and Buchanan, M (2016) What Works in Crime Prevention? Comparison and Critical Review of Three Crime Prevention Registries. *Criminology and Public Policy*, 15(3): 617–49.

Farrell, G, Phillips, C and Pease, K (1995) Like Taking Candy: Why Does Repeat Victimisation Occur? *British Journal of Criminology*, 35(3): 384–99.

Farrington, D P (1986) Age and Crime. *Crime and Justice: A Review of Research*, 7: 189–250.

Farrington, D P, Bowen, S, Buckle, A, Burns-Howell, T, Burrows, J and Speed, M (1993) An Experiment on the Prevention of Shoplifting. *Crime Prevention Studies*, 1: 93–119.

Fattah, E A (2000) Victimology: Past, Present and Future. *Criminologie*, 33(1): 17–46.

Fazel, S, Hayes, A J and Bartellas, K (2016) Mental Health of Prisoners: Prevalence, Adverse Outcomes, and Interventions. *The Lancet Psychiatry*, 3(9): 871–81.

Ford, K, Barton, E, Newbury, A, Hughes, K, Bezecky, Z, Roderick, J and Bellis, M (2019) *Understanding the Prevalence of Adverse Childhood Experiences (ACEs) in a Male Offender Population in Wales: The Prisoner ACE Survey.* Bangor: Public Health Wales.

Freeze, C (2019) Adverse Childhood Experiences and Crime. 9 April. [online] Available at: https://leb.fbi.gov/articles/featured-articles/adverse-childhood-experiences-and-crime (accessed 9 October 2023).

Freilich, J D (2007) Intelligence-Led Policing as a Framework for Responding to Terrorism. *Journal of Contemporary Criminal Justice*, 23(2): 142–58.

Gau, J M (2013) Procedural Justice and Police Legitimacy: A Test of Measurement and Structure. *American Journal of Criminal Justice*, 39(2): 187–205.

Gee, J and Button, M (2021) *The Financial Cost of Fraud 2021*. London: Crowe Global.

Goldstein, H (1979) Improving Policing: A Problem-Oriented Approach. *Crime and Delinquency*, 25(2): 236–58.

Gooch, G and Williams, M (2007) *Oxford Dictionary of Law Enforcement*. Oxford: Oxford University Press.

Goodey, J (2005) *Victims and Victimology: Research, Policy and Practice*. Harlow: Pearson Education.

Gottfredson, M and Hirschi, T (1990) *A General Theory of Crime*. Palo Alto: Stanford University Press.

Gov.uk (2012) Definition of Policing by Consent. 10 December 2012. [online] Available at: www.gov.uk/government/publications/policing-by-consent/definition-of-policing-by-consent (accessed 9 October 2023).

Graham-Kevan, N, Brooks, M, Willan, V, Lowe, M, Robinson, P, Khan, R and Bryce, J (2015) Repeat Victimisation, Retraumatisation and Victim Vulnerability. *The Open Criminology Journal*, 8: 36–48.

Gray, J M and Horvath, M A H (2018) Rape Myths in the Criminal Justice System. In Milne, E, Brennan, K, South, N and Turton, J (eds) *Women and the Criminal Justice System: Failing Victims and Offenders?* (pp 15–41). London: Palgrave Macmillan.

Grossman, J L and Friedman, L M (2014) *A Private Skirt in a Public Place: The Surprising Law of Upskirting.* Verdict. [online] Available at: https://scholarlycommons.law.hofstra.edu/cgi/viewcontent.cgi?article=1361&context=faculty_scholarship (accessed 18 September 2023).

Gul, S K (2009) An Evaluation of the Rational Choice Theory in Criminology. *Girne American University Journal of Sociology and Applied Science*, 4(8): 36–44.

Hampshire and Isle of Wight Constabulary (nd) Independent Advisory Groups and Joint Audit Committee. [online] Available at: www.hampshire.police.uk/police-forces/hampshire-constabulary/areas/careers/careers/independent-advisory-groups/ (accessed 9 October 2023).

Harcourt, B E and Ludwig, J (2006) Broken Windows: New Evidence from New York City and a Five-City Social Experiment. *Chicago Law Review*, 73(1): 271–320.

Hastings, J V and Chan, R J (2013) Target Hardening and Terrorist Signaling: The Case of Aviation Security. *Terrorism and Political Violence*, 25(5): 777–97.

Hinds, L and Murphy, K (2007) Public Satisfaction with Police: Using Procedural Justice to Improve Police Legitimacy. *The Australian and New Zealand Journal of Criminology*, 40(1): 27–42.

HMCTS (nd) Court of Appeal Criminal Division. [online] Available at: www.gov.uk/courts-tribunals/court-of-appeal-criminal-division (accessed 9 October 2023).

HMICFRS (2021a) *Disproportionate Use of Police Powers: A Spotlight on Stop and Search and the Use of Force*. London: HMICFRS.

HMICFRS (2021b) A Joint Thematic Inspection of the Police and Crown Prosecution Service's Response to Rape – Phase One: From Report to Police or CPS Decision to Take No Further Action. 16 July 2021. [online] Available at: www.justiceinspectorates.gov.uk/hmicfrs/publication-html/a-joint-thematic-inspection-of-the-police-and-crown-prosecution-services-response-to-rape-phase-one/#the-response-to-victims-when-they-report-a-rape (accessed 9 October 2023).

HMICFRS (2022) HMICFRS. 9 September 2022. [online] Available at: www.justiceinspectorates.gov.uk/hmicfrs/about-us/what-we-do/ (accessed 9 October 2023).

HMICFRS (2023) *An Inspection of How Well the Police Tackle Serious Youth Violence*. Birmingham: HMICFRS.

HMICFRS (nd) PEEL Assessments 2021/22. [online] Available at: www.justiceinspectorates.gov.uk/hmicfrs/peel-assessments/peel-assessments-2021-22/ (accessed 9 October 2023).

HM Inspectorate of Probation (2017) *The Work of Youth Offending Teams to Protect the Public*. Manchester: HM Inspectorate of Probation.

REFERENCES

HM Inspectorate of Probation (2021) Young Adults. 22 October 2021. [online] Available at: www.justiceinspectorates.gov.uk/hmiprobation/research/the-evidence-base-probation/specific-sub-groups/young-adults/ (accessed 9 October 2023).

HM Prison and Probation Service (2022) *MAPPA Guidance.* London: HM Prison and Probation Services.

HM Prison and Probation Service (2023) Offender Management Statistics Quarterly: July to September 2022. 26 January 2023. [online] Available at: www.gov.uk/government/statistics/offender-management-statistics-quarterly-july-to-september-2022/offender-management-statistics-quarterly-july-to-september-2022 (accessed 9 October 2023).

Hobson, J, Lynch, K, Payne, B and Ellis, L (2018) Are Police-Led Social Crime Prevention Initiatives Effective? A Process and Outcome Evaluation of a UK Youth Intervention. *International Criminal Justice Review*, 31(3): 1–22.

Home Office (2004) *Crimes against Students: Emerging Lessons for Reducing Student Victimisation.* London: Home Office.

Home Office (2022) *Home Office Counting Rules 2022/3.* London: Home Office.

Hood, R, Shute, S, Feilizer, M and Wilcox, A (2002) Sex Offenders Emerging from Long-Term Imprisonment: A Study of Their Long-Term Reconviction Rates and of Parole Board Members' Judgements of Their Risk. *British Journal of Criminology*, 42(2): 371–94.

Hope, T (2005) The New Local Governance of Community Safety in England and Wales. *Canadian Journal of Criminology and Criminal Justice*, 47(2): 369–87.

Hutton, G, Cox, A, Gold, E and Connor, P (2022) *Blackstone's Police Manual 2023: Volume 3 – General Police Duties.* Oxford: Oxford University Press.

Independent Custody Visiting Association (nd) Purpose. [online] Available at: https://icva.org.uk/purpose/#purpose-volunteering (accessed 9 October 2023).

Independent Police Complaints Commission (2009) *IPCC Report into the Contact between Fiona Pilkington and Leicestershire Constabulary 2004–2007.* London: Independent Police Complaints Commission.

Jacobs, B A and Cherbonneau, M (2019) Carjacking and the Management of Natural Surveillance. *Journal of Criminal Justice*, 61(March–April): 40–7.

Janowitz, M (1975) Sociological Theory and Social Control. *American Journal of Sociology*, 81(1): 82–108.

REFERENCES

Johnson, S D (2008) Repeat Burglary Victimisation: A Tale of Two Theories. *Journal of Experimental Criminology*, 4: 215–40.

Keel, R (2019) Rational Choice and Deterrence Theory. 26 November 2019. [online] Available at: www.umsl.edu/~keelr/200/ratchoc.html (accessed 9 October 2023).

Kempa, M and Johnston, L (2005) Challenges and Prospects for the Development of Inclusive Plural Policing in Britain: Overcoming Political and Conceptual Obstacles. *The Australian and New Zealand Journal of Criminology*, 38(2): 181–91.

Kendall, J (2022) Custody Visiting: The Watchdog That Didn't Bark. *Criminology and Criminal Justice*, 22(1): 115–31.

Keningale, P (2020) The National Intelligence Model. 26 May 2020. [online] Available at: https://bscpolicingnetwork.wordpress.com/2022/05/31/the-national-intelligence-model-the-barriers-to-its-success/ (accessed 9 October 2023).

Konkel, R H, Ratkowski, D and Tapp, S N (2019) The Effects of Physical, Social and Housing Disorder on Neighborhood Crime: A Contemporary Test of Broken Windows Theory. *International Journal of Geo-Information*, 8(12): 583–601.

Koper, C S (1995) Just Enough Police Presence: Reducing Crime and Disorderly Behaviour by Optimizing Patrol Time in Crime Hot Spots. *Justice Quarterly*, 12(4): 649–72.

Kuo, F E and Sullivan, W C (2001) Environment and Crime in the Inner City: Does Vegetation Reduce Crime? *Environment and Behavior*, 33(3): 343–67.

Lombroso, C (2006) *Criminal Man [5th Edition] Translated by Mary Gibson and Nicole Hahn Rafter.* London: Duke University Press.

London Irish (nd) HITZ. [online] Available at: www.london-irish.com/foundation/hitz/565/ (accessed 9 October 2023).

Lord Scarman (1981) *The Scarman Report.* London: Her Majesty's Stationery Office.

Loveday, B (2017) Still Plodding Along? The Police Response to the Changing Profile of Crime in England and Wales. *International Journal of Police Science and Management*, 19(2): 1–9.

Macpherson, W (1999) *The Stephen Lawrence Inquiry.* London: Home Office.

Maguire, M (2008) Criminal Investigation and Crime Control. In Newburn, T (ed) *Handbook of Policing* (pp 430–64). Cullompton: Willan Publishing.

Maguire, M and John, T (2006) Intelligence Led Policing, Managerialism and Community Engagement: Competing Priorities and the Role of the National Intelligence Model in the UK. *Policing and Society*, 16(1): 67–85.

Mawby, R I and Smith, K (2013) Accounting for the Police: The New Police and Crime Commissioners in England and Wales. *The Police Journal*, 86(2): 143–57.

Mazerolle, L, Bennett, S, Davis, J, Sargeant, E and Manning, M (2015) Procedural Justice and Police Legitimacy: A Systematic Review of the Research Evidence. *Journal of Experimental Criminology*, 9(3): 245–74.

McAlinden, A M (2005) The Use of 'Shame' with Sexual Offenders. *British Journal of Criminology*, 45(3): 373–94.

McGlynn, C and Rackley, E (2017) Why 'Upskirting' Needs to Be Made a Sex Crime. 15 August 2017. [online] Available at: https://theconversation.com/why-upskirting-needs-to-be-made-a-sex-crime-82357 (accessed 9 October 2023).

McGlynn, C, Westmarland, N and Godden, N (2012) 'I Just Wanted Him to Hear Me': Sexual Violence and the Possibilities of Restorative Justice. *Journal of Law and Society*, 39(2): 213–40.

McInnes, R (2020) General Election 2019: Turnout. 7 January 2020. [online] Available at: https://commonslibrary.parliament.uk/general-election-2019-turnout/ (accessed 9 October 2023).

McLaughlin, E and Johansen, A (2002) A Force for Change? The Prospects for Applying Restorative Justice to Citizen Complaints against the Police in England and Wales. *British Journal of Criminology*, 42(3): 635–53.

McMurran, M (2007) What Works in Substance Misuse Treatments for Offenders? *Criminal Behaviour and Mental Health*, 17(4): 225–33.

Ministry of Justice (2019a) 'Upskirting' Now a Specific Crime as Bill Receives Royal Assent. 12 February 2019. [online] Available at: www.gov.uk/government/news/upskirting-now-a-specific-crime-after-bill-receives-royal-assent (accessed 9 October 2023).

Ministry of Justice (2019b) 'Upskirting' Law Comes into Force. 12 April 2019. [online] Available at: www.gov.uk/government/news/upskirting-law-comes-into-force (accessed 9 October 2023).

Miro, F (2014) Routine Activity Theory. In Miller, J M (ed) *The Encyclopedia of Theoretical Criminology* (pp 1–7). Chichester: Wiley-Blackwell.

My Local Bobby (2022) About Us. [online] Available at: https://mylocalbobby.co.uk/about-us/ (accessed 9 October 2023).

Newburn, T (2007) *Criminology*. Cullompton: Willan Publishing.

NHS (2018) Fraudulent Prescriptions: A Serious Risk to the NHS. 14 August 2018. [online] Available at: https://cfa.nhs.uk/about-nhscfa/latest-news/fraudulent-prescriptions-serious-risk-to-nhs (accessed 9 October 2023).

NHS: Counter Fraud Authority (2018) *Business Plan 2018–19*. London: NHS.

NHS: Counter Fraud Authority (2022) NHS: Counter Fraud Authority. [online] Available at: https://cfa.nhs.uk/ (accessed 30 October 2023).

Nickolls, L (2022) Police Vetting: How It Works and Calls for Change. 11 November. [online] Available at: https://commonslibrary.parliament.uk/police-vetting-how-it-works-and-calls-for-change/ (accessed 9 October 2023).

O'Connell, H (2017) *What Happens in the Shadows: Streetlights and How They Relate to Crime*. Houston: Rice Kinder Institute for Urban Research.

Office for National Statistics (2013) *An Overview of Sexual Offending in England and Wales*. London: Office for National Statistics.

Office for National Statistics (2017) *Overview of Bicycle Theft: England and Wales*. London: Office for National Statistics.

Office for National Statistics (2022) *Crime in England and Wales: Quality and Methodology Information*. London: Office for National Statistics.

O'Leary, M (2011) Modeling Criminal Distance Decay. *Cityscape*, 13(3): 161–98.

Park, E, Burgess, E W and McKenzie, R D (1925) *The City*. Chicago: University of Chicago Press.

Parole Board (nd) About Us. [online] Available at: www.gov.uk/government/organisations/parole-board/about (accessed 9 October 2023).

Petrunik, M (1980) The Rise and Fall of 'Labelling Theory': The Construction and Destruction of a Sociological Strawman. *The Canadian Journal of Sociology*, 5(3): 213–33.

Pierce, M, Hayhust, K, Bird, S M, Hickman, M, Seddon, T, Dunn, G and Millar, T (2015) Quantifying Crime Associated with Drug Use among a Large Cohort of Sanctioned Offenders in England and Wales. *Drug and Alcohol Dependence*, 155: 52–9.

Piza, E L, Welsh, B C, Farrington, D P and Thomas, A L (2019) *CCTV Surveillance for Crime Prevention: Systematic Review with Meta-Analysis*. New York: City University of New York.

Police Crime Prevention Initiatives (2022) What Is CSAS and RSAS? [online] Available at: www.policecsas.com/ (accessed 9 October 2023).

Poyner, B (1993) What Works in Crime Prevention: An Overview of Evaluations. *Crime Prevention Studies*, 1: 7–34.

Premiership Rugby (nd) Our Hitz Programme. [online] Available at: www.premiershiprugby.com/community/hitz/ (accessed 9 October 2023).

Probation Service (nd) About Us. [online] Available at: www.gov.uk/government/organisations/probation-service/about (accessed 9 October 2023).

Ramos, J and Torgler, B (2012) Are Academics Messy? Testing the Broken Windows Theory with a Field Experiment in the Work Environment. *Review of Law and Economics*, 8(3): 563–77.

Ratcliffe, J H (2002) Intelligence-Led Policing and the Problems of Turning Rhetoric into Practice. *Policing and Society*, 12(1): 53–66.

Ratcliffe, J H (2016) *Intelligence-Led Policing*. Abingdon: Routledge.

Ratcliffe, J H, Perenzin, A and Sorg, E T (2016) Operation Thumbs Down: A Quasi-Experimental Evaluation of an FBI Gang Takedown in South Central Los Angeles. *Policing: An International Journal*, 40(2): 442–58.

Recipero (2022) About the Immobilise System. [online] Available at: www.immobilise.com/about (accessed 9 October 2023).

Reisig, M D and Lloyd, C (2009) Procedural Justice, Police Legitimacy and Helping the Police Fight Crime: Results from a Survey of Jamaican Adolescents. *Police Quarterly*, 12(1): 42–62.

Rengert, F G, Piquero, A R and Jones, P R (1999) Distance Decay Reexamined. *Criminology*, 37(2): 427–46.

Reynes, B W (2013) Online Routines and Identity Theft Victimization: Further Expanding Routine Activity Theory beyond Direct-Contact Offenses. *Journal of Research in Crime and Delinquency*, 50(2): 216–38.

Rock, P (2007) Caesare Lombroso as a Signal Criminologist. *Criminology and Criminal Justice*, 7(2): 117–33.

Rosenfeld, R, Deckard, M J and Blackburn, E (2014) The Effects of Directed Patrol and Self-Initiated Enforcement on Firearm Violence: A Randomized Controlled Study of Hot Spot Policing. *Criminology*, 52(3): 428–49.

Savage, S P (2007) *Police Reform: Forces for Change.* Oxford: Oxford University Press.

Schaap, D (2018) *The Police, the Public, and the Pursuit of Trust.* The Hague: Eleven International Publishing.

Seneviratne, M (2004) Policing the Police in the United Kingdom. *Policing and Society*, 14(4): 329–47.

Shannon, I (2020) Democratic Oversight and Political Direction of Chief Police Officers in England and Wales: Implications for Police Legitimacy. *Policing*, 15(2): 912–26.

Sherman, L W, Gartin, P R and Buerger, M E (1989) Hot Spots of Predatory Crime: Routine Activities and the Criminology of Place. *Criminology*, 27(1): 27–55.

Shorrock, S, McManus, M and Kirby, S (2020) Profile of Repeat Victimisation within Multi-Agency Referrals. *International Review of Victimology*, 26(3): 332–43.

Sleath, E and Bull, R (2017) Police Perceptions of Rape Victims and the Impact on Case Decision Making: A Systematic Review. *Aggression and Violent Behaviour*, 34(May): 102–12.

Sloper, R (2022) Almost 40 Grimsby Homes Warned over 'Messing up Streets'. 16 March 2022. [online] Available at: www.grimsbytelegraph.co.uk/news/grimsby-news/almost-40-grimsby-homes-warned-6813160 (accessed 9 October 2023).

Smartwater (2020) Partnering with Law Enforcement. [online] Available at: https://swt.smartwater.com/law-enforcement/ (accessed 9 October 2023).

Smith, D J (2007) Crime and the Life Course. In Maguire M, Morgan, R and Reiner, R (eds) *The Oxford Handbook of Criminology [Fourth Edition]* (pp 641–86). Oxford: Oxford University Press.

Sucic, I and Karlovic, R (2017) Community Policing in Support of Social Cohesion. In Akhgar, B and Markarian, G (eds) *Community Police – a European Perspective: Strategies, Best Practices and Guidelines* (pp 7–20). Cham: Springer.

Supreme Court (2022) Role of The Supreme Court. [online] Available at: www.supremecourt.uk/about/role-of-the-supreme-court.html (accessed 9 October 2023).

Telep, C W, Mitchell, J R and Weisburd, D (2012) How Much Time Should the Police Spend at Crime Hot Spots? Answers from a Police Agency Directed Randomized Field Trial in Sacramento, California. *Justice Quarterly*, 31(5): 905–33.

Terer, K and Brown, R (2014) Effective Drink Driving Prevention and Enforcement Strategies: Approaches to Improving Practice. *Trends and Issues in Crime and Criminal Justice*, 472: 1.

Tett, L, Anderson, K, Mcneill, F, Overy, K and Sparks, R (2012) Learning, Rehabilitation and the Arts in Prison. *Studies in the Education of Adults*, 44(2): 171–85.

Tilley, N (2008) Modern Approaches to Policing: Community, Problem-Oriented and Intelligence-Led. In Newburn, T (ed) *Handbook of Policing* (pp 373–403). Cullompton: Willan Publishing.

Tseloni, A and Pease, K (2003) Repeat Personal Victimisation: 'Boosts' or 'Flags'? *British Journal of Criminology*, 43(1): 196–212.

Turanovic, J J and Pratt, T C (2014) 'Can't Stop, Won't Stop': Self-Control, Risky Lifestyles, and Repeat Victimization. *Journal of Quantitative Criminology*, 30(1): 29–56.

Tyler, T R (2004) Procedural Justice. In Sarat, A (ed) *The Blackwell Companion to Law and Society* (pp 435–52). Oxford: Blackwell Publishing.

UK Parliament (nd) Public Bills. [online] Available at: www.parliament.uk/about/how/laws/bills/public/ (accessed 9 October 2023).

Verhoeven, M, van Gestel, B, de Jong, D and Kleemans, E (2015) Relationships between Suspects and Victims of Sex Trafficking: Exploitation of Prostitutes and Domestic Violence Parallels in Dutch Trafficking Cases. *European Journal on Criminal Policy and Research*, 21(1): 49–64.

Victim Support (nd) What Is a Crime? [online] Available at: www.victimsupport.org.uk/crime-info/what-crime/ (accessed 9 October 2023).

Von Hentig, H (1940) Remarks on the Interaction of Perpetrator and Victim. *Journal of Criminal Law and Criminology (1931–1951)*, 31(3): 303–9.

Walklate, S (1990) Researching Victims of Crime: Critical Victimology. *Social Justice*, 17(3): 25–42.

Weaver, B and Fraser, A (2022) The Social Dynamics of Group Offending. *Theoretical Criminology*, 26(2): 264–84.

Weiss, I (2001) The Ideology, Policy and Practice of Adult Probation Service in Israel. *British Journal of Social Work*, 31(5): 775–89.

Wenzel, M and Okimoto, T G (2016) Retributive Justice. In Sabbagh, C and Schmitt, M (eds) *Handbook of Social Justice Theory and Research* (pp 237–56). New York: Springer.

West Yorkshire Police (nd) The 10 Principles of Crime Prevention. [online] Available at: www.westyorkshire.police.uk/advice/10-principles-crime-prevention/10-principles-crime-prevention/10-principles-crime-prevention (accessed 9 October 2023).

Williams, B (2023) *Policing Mental Health, Vulnerability and Risk*. St Albans: Critical Publishing.

Wilson, J Q and Kelling, G L (1982) The Police and Neighborhood Safety: Broken Windows. *The Atlantic Monthly*, March: 29–38.

Wolff, K T and Baglivio, M T (2016) Adverse Childhood Experiences, Negative Emotionality and Pathways to Juvenile Recidivism. *Crime and Delinquency*, 63(12): 1–27.

Wolfgang, M E (1958) *Patterns in Criminal Homicide*. Philadephia: University of Pennsylvania Press.

Wolfgang, M E (1961) Pioneers in Criminology: Cesare Lombroso (1835–1909). *Journal of Criminal Law, Criminology and Police Science*, 52(4): 361–91.

Wolfgang, M E, Figlio, R M and Sellin, T (1972) *Delinquency in a Birth Cohort*. Chicago: The University of Chicago Press.

Wood, J and Kemshall, H (2007) *The Operation and Experience of Multi-Agency Public Protection Arrangements (MAPPA)*. London: Home Office.

Wood, J, Swanson, J, Burris, S and Gilbert, A (2011) *Police Interventions with Persons Affected by Mental Illnesses: A Critical Review of Global Thinking and Practice*. New Brunswick: Centre for Behavioural Health Services and Criminal Justice Research.

Yarwood, R and Edwards, B (1995) Voluntary Action in Rural Areas: The Case of Neighbourhood Watch. *Journal of Rural Studies*, 11(4): 447–59.

Yokum, D, Ravishankar, A and Coppock, A (2019) A Randomized Control Trial Evaluating the Effects of Police Body-Worn Cameras. *PNAS*, 116(21): 10329–32.

Zimbardo, P G (1970) *A Social-Psychological Analysis of Vandalism: Making Sense out of Senseless Violence*. Stanford: Stanford University CA Dept of Psychology.

INDEX

access control, and crime prevention, 98–9
accommodation status, and offending, 27
activity support, and crime prevention, 107
adverse childhood experiences (ACEs), and offending, 16, 27–9, 136–7
age-offending curve, 24–6
alcohol use, and offending, 27
Authorised Professional Practice (APP), 81
average offenders, 43

Betari's Box, 49
Bhopal gas tragedy (1984), 18
body-worn devices, 82, 84, 139
British Transport Police (BTP), 11
Brixton riots (1981), 54, 127
broken windows theory, 31–3, 106, 137
buffer zones, 42

CCTV surveillance, 99, 100
Chicago School model, 40–1
citizen input, in community policing, 126
citizen oversight, 85–6
    independent advisory groups (IAGs), 86
    lay custody visitors, 86–7
citizen participation in proceedings, 48

Code of Ethics, 81
cognitive behavioural therapy (CBT), 69
College of Policing, 81–3, 108
community policing, 125
    broad function, 126
    and citizen input, 126
    implementation of, 128–9
    importance of, 127–8
    lack of engagement, 129–30
    partnerships, 128–9
    personal service, 127
    poor status within policing, 130–2
    positive interaction, 128
    problem solving, 129
commuters, 43
courts, 67–8, 138
CPTED (crime prevention through environmental design), 105–6
crime
    dark figure of, 9, 25, 135
    meaning and definitions for, 6–8
    measurement of, 8–12
    reasons for committing, 6
    singular incident measurement, 11
crime prevention, 94
    and access control, 98–9
    and activity support, 107
    CPTED (crime prevention through

environmental design), 105–6
    and criminology, 108–9
    and deflecting offenders principle, 103
    and environmental change, 101
    and image and maintenance, 106–7
    and 'increasing the chances of being caught' principle, 101–2
    interventions, evaluation of, 107–8, 140
    and means reduction, 97
    and payoff reduction, 97–8
    principles of, 94–103, 108–9, 139–40
    and rule setting, 101
    situational, 103–5
    and surveillance, 99–101
    and target hardening, 95–6
    and target removal, 96–7, 140
    and territoriality, 106
crime recording, 20
Crime Survey for England and Wales (CSEW), 9–11, 135
crime triangle, 38, 116
crimesolutions.gov, 108
criminal justice system (CJS), 20, 60, 63–4
    courts, 67–8, 138
    Crown Prosecution Service (CPS), 64–6
    offender management, 70–2

parole board, 69–70
police service, 64
prison service, 68–9
probation, 68
and social control, 76
critical victimology, 18
Crown Prosecution Service (CPS), 64–6
CSAS scheme, 61

deflecting offenders principle, 103
distance decay theory, 42–3, 137
diversion programmes, 103
domestic abuse/violence, 12–13, 18
drink driving testing, 36
drug and substance misuse, and offending, 27, 28

education level, and offending, 27
environmental change, and crime prevention, 101
environmental criminology, 40
event dependency, and victimisation, 15
Everard, Sarah, murder of, 77
evidential test, 65, 138

full code test, 65, 66

general deterrence, 35–6
general population prisons, 68
geographic profiling, 43
guilty mind, 30

Helping with Enquiries – Tackling Crime Effectively, 121
HITZ programme, 72
HM Courts and Tribunal Service (HMTCS), 67
HM Inspectorate of Constabulary and Fire and Rescue Services (HMICFRS), 9, 80–1, 121, 139
Home Office Counting Rules (HOCR), 8–9
hot spot policing, 112–15, 140
 crime displacement, 115
 response times, 115

image and maintenance, 106–7
Immobilise, 97
incapacitation, 35
incapacitation, and offending, 36–7
'increasing the chances of being caught' principle, 101–2
independent advisory groups (IAGs), 86
intelligence-led policing, 121–2
 implementation challenges, 125
 information challenges, 124–5
 National Intelligence Model (NIM), 122–4
 oversimplifying the role of policing, 125

judicial precedent, 67
just deserts, 35

Kent Police, 121

labelling theory, 33–4
LAC (looked after child), and offending, 27
law, creation of, 87–9
lay custody visitors, 86–7
Lombroso's theory, 30–1
long-term prisons, 68

Macpherson report, 128
MAPPA, 70–1, 73, 138
marauders, 43
means reduction, and crime prevention, 97, 140
media, influence of, 77–8
mens rea, 30
mobile phones, locating offenders using, 44
modus operandi (MO), 8
money needs, locating offenders using, 44
multi-agency safeguarding hub (MASH), 13
murder cases, 17
My Local Bobby, 61

National Intelligence Model (NIM), 122–4
 and problem profile, 122
 and strategic assessment, 123
 and subject profile, 122
 and tactical assessment, 123
National Police Chiefs Council (NPCC), 19
natural surveillance, 99–100, 101
neighbourhood watch schemes, 100–1
NHS (National Health Service), and target removal, 96

offenders and offending, 24. *See also* victims–offenders relationship
  and adverse childhood experiences (ACEs), 27–9, 136–7
  and age, 24–6
  biological reasons for, 30–1
  broken windows theory, 31–3
  Chicago School model, 40–1
  deflecting principle, 103
  disadvantages, 26–9
  distance decay theory, 42–3, 137
  drug and substance misuse and, 28
  environmental factors, 40–3
  incapacitation, 36–7
  labelling theory, 33–4
  locating offenders, 43–4, 137
  management of, 70–2
  and MAPPA, 70–1, 73, 138
  psychological reasons, 35–40
  rational choice theory, 35–8
  revolving door of offending, 25
  routine activity theory, 38–40
  self-reported, 27
  sexual offenders, 34
  sociological theories of, 31–4
  specific deterrence, 36
  and youth offending teams (YOT), 71–2
Operation Bluestone, 16
Operation Thumbs Down, 124
out of court disposals, 64

parole board, 69–70
payoff reduction, and crime prevention, 97–8
Peelian principles, 48, 76, 126
pluralised policing, 61–2
police accountability, 81–3, 84
police and crime commissioners (PCC), 78–80
Police Community Support Officers (PCSOs), 61, 114
police complaints, 83–5
police constables, 62
Police Effectiveness, Efficiency and Legitimacy (PEEL) assessments, 80
police recorded crime, 8–9
police service, 64
policing, role of, 61–3
politics, 76, 139
positive interaction, 141
positivist victimology, 17–18
pre-sentence reports (PSRs), 68
prison service, 68–9
probation service, 68, 70
problem profile, 122
problem-oriented policing, 115–16, 129
  lack of engagement, 121
  no assessment of impact, 120–1
  poor analysis, 120
  SARA model, 116–20

procedural justice, 137–8
  citizen participation in proceedings, 48
  components of, 48
  decision making, neutrality in, 49
  definition of, 48
  dignity and respect, 49–50
  fairness, 53
  importance to policing, 51–2
  related issues, 52–5
  trustworthy motives, 50
'Project Restore', New Zealand, 19
public interactions, importance of, 53–5
public interest test, 65, 73, 138
punishments, 70

railway crime measurement, 11–12
rape cases, 15–16
rational choice theory, 35–8, 108, 113
rehabilitation, 70
repeat victimisation
  demographic factor, 14
  domestic abuse, 12–13
  and event dependency, 15
  external factors, 13–14
  and self-control, 13
  and trauma-based response, 13
  vulnerabilities, 13–15
restorative justice (RJ), 18–20, 136
retributive justice, 35, 37
revolving door of offending, 25

routine activity theory, 38–40, 113, 136
RSAS scheme, 61
rule setting, and crime prevention, 101

SARA model, 116, 140
　analysis, 116–17
　assessment, 118
　response, 117–18
　scanning, 116
self-control behaviour, and victimisation, 13
sexual offenders, 24, 29, 34, 70
shoplifting, prevention of, 102
situational crime prevention, 103–5
Smartwater, 102
social control, 60–1, 138
　and criminal justice system (CJS), 76
　and policing, 61–3
social media, locating offenders using, 44

strategic assessment, 123
street lighting, 101, 140
subject profile, 122
supreme court, 67
surveillance, and crime prevention, 99–101
suspects, tracking down, 43–4, 137

tactical assessment, 123, 141
target hardening, and crime prevention, 95–6
target removal, and crime prevention, 96–7, 140
territoriality, and crime prevention, 106
therapeutic surveillance, 71
trauma-based response, 13

upskirting incident, 88

Victim Support, 6
victimisation, 135–6. See also repeat victimisation

victimology, 17
　critical, 18
　positivist, 17–18
victims
　repeat victimisation. See repeat victimisation
　safeguarding, 20
victims–offenders relationship. See also offenders and offending
　in adverse childhood experiences (ACEs) cases, 16
　in rape cases, 15–16
　in murder cases, 17

What Works Centre for Crime Prevention, 108

youth offenders, prisons, 68
youth offending teams (YOTs), 71–2, 73